W9-BIF-926

About Thriveworks

Thriveworks is a counseling practice with 85+ locations across the US and an important mission: to help people live happy, successful lives. We accomplish this mission by providing clients premium mental health services, with outstanding providers, exceptional customer service, and valuable life improvement resources. One of those resources is this book, which was written to help people begin the journey toward recovery (e.g., "Leaving Depression Behind"). We hope this resource proves helpful in your life and that it encourages you to obtain greater health, happiness, and success. To learn more about Thriveworks, or to get connected with a licensed mental health professional near you, visit Thriveworks.com

Contents

I

Start Here

Let's get straight to it: you're not feeling so great. You're actually feeling pretty crappy, and you don't know what to do about it. That's why (even though you don't know who we are) you've picked up this book and are willing to take a swing at something that might help. First off, we want to commend you. You've taken on the difficult task of dealing with depression, without having much say in the matter. Secondly, if you're like most of the people we see in counseling, you're doing a lot better than you think. You're living, you're managing, you're hanging in there… but that's just not going to cut it for you anymore. You're reading this right now because you want to do better, be better, and feel better. So that's what you're going to get from us: a how-to do better, be better, and feel better.

You are not untreatable or incurable. Everything we discuss in this book will help you better manage all that comes with depression—from feeling sad or anxious to losing interest in the things and people you love. Don't believe us? Keep reading, and we'll prove it. We're here to guide you through the journey—whether you're a new mom experiencing post-partum depression, someone who's sick of feeling like crap in the winter months, or an average person in need of some advice and inspiration.

This is a "Choose Your Path" book, which means you decide which sections you read and which sections you skip, based on how you feel and what you're seeking. Hopefully, the journey you'll take through the pages ahead—whichever pages those might be—will help you move forward in your life and toward happiness.

We can't promise this book will cure you of your depression (if we did, Dr. AJ would lose his license). But we can and do promise each page was carefully written to help. And because you've picked up this book, we know you believe that. Or at least you want to believe, and that's good enough for now.

◊ **To learn about the lies you've been telling yourself, flip to the next page**

◊ **To read about the most common form of depression, turn to page 21**

◊ **To read about how your feelings rule your life, turn to page 61**

2

The Lies We Tell Ourselves

"I'm fine," you say with a quick flash of a smile. *Just get them off my back.*

"Huh, I never got your call." As you pretend to sort through your phone, confused.

"I already have plans." *Plans with Netflix and Hulu.*

Sound familiar? Most people would agree that these white lies are virtually harmless.

But what about the lies we tell <u>ourselves</u>?

If we're depressed, we're lying to ourselves on a daily basis. We just don't know or realize we're doing it. Imagine you're getting ready to go out with friends. You've spent an hour on your hair, 30 minutes picking out the perfect outfit, and another 20 scrutinizing yourself in the mirror. Still, you think to yourself, "I look awful, I should just stay in." This is a prime example of negative thinking—a pattern of telling ourselves harmful lies. Such thinking can make a good day bad and a bad day worse. However, we can combat our negative thinking and, in turn, live much happier lives. Consider the following:

A man is walking in the park when a 6-year-old boy runs up and kicks him in the shins. Without a single word, the boy turns and runs away. The man berates himself over the bizarre occurrence. "I'm such a loser," he says to himself. "Even kids don't like me." He turns around, head held low, and walks back toward home. A little while later, the same kid runs up to a different man in the park, kicks him in the shins and again hurries away. This man erupts with laughter and says, "What a rambunctious little kid! That was the funniest thing I've seen all day."

The first man feels sad and defeated. The second man is happy and humored. A third individual might react with anger, and a fourth might feel scared. They've all experienced the same situation but their thoughts about the event led to very different feelings. We all want to be the person who turned to positivity and humor, but when we're depressed, we often wind up more like the first man, feeling defective and rejected. We call these lies we tell ourselves "mental deceptions." Here's a list of them:

Deception:	What It Is:	Example:
All-Or-Nothing Thinking	You see everything as either black or white. If you fall short of perfect, you see yourself as a total failure.	During a job interview, you stumble over the answer to one of about 30 questions. The rest of the interview went exceedingly well; however, you focus solely on the one question where you struggled. You call yourself a failure.
Overgeneralization	You mistake a single negative event for a never-ending negative pattern.	You stay at work late and are "rewarded" with a parking ticket. The sign on the street reads: No parking after 5 p.m. "This crap always happens," you think to yourself.
Mental Filter	You pick out a single defeat and then dwell on it. Your vision of reality becomes darkened, like the single drop of ink that colors an entire bottle of water.	You're out with friends and everybody's enjoying themselves. Everybody except for you. All you can think about is the dismissive look the waiter gave you when he took your order. You feel deflated.

Deception:	What It Is:	Example:
Disqualifying the Positive	You dismiss positive experiences by insisting they "don't count" for some reason.	"You did such an awesome job! What an amazing performance," your friend says as you walk off stage. But instead of acknowledging your success, you convince yourself that your friend is just trying to be nice.
Mind Reading	You conclude that someone is reacting negatively to you, even though you don't know what they're actually thinking.	It's been a while since you've heard from your brother, and you start to wonder why. You conclude that he's angry with you because you couldn't make it to his birthday party last month.
Fortune Telling	You expect that things will turn out badly.	"Come on, you're going to have a great time!" your friend says. You insist your blind date is going to be horrible.

Deception:	What It Is:	Example:
Catastrophizing	You exaggerate the importance of things, such as your mistakes or a competitor's achievements, to your own detriment.	You see on Instagram that an old colleague just received a promotion. "Ugh! Everyone's dreams are coming true except for mine," you think to yourself.
Minimization	You shrink positive things until they appear inconsequential.	Your coworker compliments you on your hair when you walk into work. Instead of thanking her and feeling flattered by the compliment, you list everything you don't like about your hair.
Should Statements	You try to motivate yourself with "shoulds" and "shouldn'ts" ("musts" and "oughts" are also offenders). The emotional consequence is guilt.	You jolt awake at the alarm you set for 6 a.m., but then you just lie there. "I should really go to the gym," you say to yourself. A few hours later, you've yet to work out and you're overwhelmed with guilt.

Emotional Reasoning	You assume that your emotions (often negative) reflect the way things actually are: "I feel it, so it must be true."	Your date insists on picking up the check, and you thank him profusely. When you get home, you look back on the night and decide you thanked him one too many times… embarrassment takes over. "I'm so embarrassing! He must have been so annoyed with me!"
Labeling	Instead of describing your error, you attach a negative label to yourself such as, "I'm a loser." Labeling involves describing an event with language that is highly colored and emotionally loaded.	You get to work and realize you left your wallet at home. Instead of acknowledging it as a simple mistake, you say, "I'm such an idiot!"

Personalization	You see yourself as the cause of some negative external event that you were not, in fact, primarily responsible for.	When you walk into work, a coworker tells you the bad news: your friend was fired. Your mind goes into overdrive. "I should have helped him with that project. It's my fault for not stopping him from leaving early on Friday."

Can you think of examples in your life where you have used any of the deceptions we just discussed? I'm definitely guilty of mind reading and fortune telling (Taylor, here). For instance, last week I concluded that a friend was ignoring me because she hadn't answered any of my texts or phone calls. In reality, she had dropped her phone in the toilet. This is mind reading at its finest.

Now, it's your turn. Take a few minutes to think about the deceptions you engage in. **Feel free to write them down below, followed by an example or two:**

Deception: _____

_____

Example: _____

_____

Deception: _____

_____

Example: _____

_____

Are you starting to see how the way you think will affect the way you feel? It's easy to get into a bad habit of negative thinking, but—with practice—you can develop the ability to identify your mental deceptions and replace them with more helpful, more honest thoughts about yourself and the world around you. This is, perhaps, step one in your journey to leave depression behind.

◊ **To learn more about how your thoughts affect the way you feel, turn the page**

◊ **If you've recently gone through a breakup, flip to page 55**

◊ **To learn about anxiety, depression's partner in crime, turn to page 69**

3

The Reality Is...

Often, we attribute our emotions, our moods, and our issues to things that have happened to us...

"I'm upset because my girlfriend is ignoring me."

"I'm hurt because my friends don't want to hang out with me."

"I'm depressed because my coworkers don't like me."

We insist that we're cursed or unlucky and we're tempted to wallow in our own pity. But we (you!) are not that powerless. Our feelings are not the consequence of what has happened to us; instead, they are the product of our *beliefs* about what has happened to us. Albert Ellis, an American psychologist who is best known for his contributions to a form of therapy called cognitive behavioral therapy (CBT), created a simple equation for understanding this notion: A+B=C.[1]

A = The thing that happened
B = Beliefs about the thing that happened
C = How you feel

You're not upset because your girlfriend is ignoring you, you're upset because you *think* she's ignoring you. And, you also think, if she's ignoring you then she's going to dump you. Then, you reason, it's going to be horrible to see her with someone else. Also, you're not going to find someone else you like as much as her. AND you might be alone for a long, long time. (Yeah, who wouldn't feel depressed with thoughts like that). However, regardless, of the situation, you are in control of your thinking. How about this for a productive thought: "I haven't heard from my girlfriend in a while. It's probably nothing. However, if I'm not hearing from her because she doesn't like me anymore, I'll be okay. I'll find someone else. I'm worthy of love, and I'm always going to be okay." Let's dig into another scenario:

Sansa is stuck waiting in line at the DMV for over an hour. When she finally gets to the front desk, she tries to register her vehicle, but can't because she lacks a pertinent form. What's more, Sansa called ahead and asked which forms

---

1   McLeod, S. (2008). Cognitive behavioral therapy. Simply Psychology. Retrieved from https://simplypsychology.org/cognitive-therapy.html

she needed to bring with her, so as to ensure she got everything settled today. But because she was misinformed by a DMV representative, she'll have to return at a later time and wait in line... again.

Sansa states that she's angry because she has had to wait too long at the DMV and also because she was misinformed by the DMV representative—probably on purpose. Furthermore, she begins to think, "I shouldn't have to do this. My husband should!" To make matters even worse, she drives home in a fury and soon gets into a screaming match with her husband.

According to the ABC Model mentioned previously, Sansa isn't upset because of what has happened (A). She's upset because of her beliefs (B), which led to how she feels (C). Basically, we all suffer from irrational beliefs and can benefit from both identifying and modifying those beliefs. Now, let's identify Sansa's mental deceptions:

1. I should not have to wait in line for over an hour!

2. People should be capable of providing me with correct information.

3. The representative on the phone gave me bad information on purpose.

4. Since my husband has a less demanding schedule, he should go to the DMV—not me!

5. This has ruined my entire day.

Can you see how Sansa's beliefs are fueling the way she acts and feels? Let's replace these unhelpful thoughts with thoughts that are more productive. How about these:

1. It was inconvenient to wait in line for such a long time, but it's not the end of the world. In fact, I actually had a rare opportunity to read my book and daydream.

2. Nobody's perfect—I forgive the representative for giving me the wrong information.

3. I'm sure she didn't mean to steer me in the wrong direction; everyone makes mistakes! She probably wasn't trained properly.

4. I'm glad my husband didn't have to do this today. He's had a rough week.

5. Things didn't work out the way I wanted today, but life is still good.

These five positive thoughts would result in much less emotional turmoil. Now, is it possible that the person Sansa spoke with on the phone gave her poor information on purpose? That her husband has more time to wait at the DMV than she does? And that the person at the counter could have registered her car anyway? Sure! But there's no evidence to support it, and it doesn't benefit Sansa to think negatively.

Let's take everything we have learned about thoughts and feelings so far and put them into practice. You'll find a mood log on the next few pages where you can review/record an event in which you experienced negative thoughts and feelings. You will first identify those negative thoughts and feelings, and then work on improving them.

We know, this might be difficult until you get the hang of it. Here's a little tidbit that will help: When you're emotionally charged, your mental deceptions feel more real than they are; but when you calm down, you can recognize them as lies. That's where the "How true? Then/Now" column comes into play. In the heat of the moment, your negative thought might feel 100% true. But when you take a step back, you'll realize this thought was silly, and there's only a 15% chance of it being true. Keep this in mind as you fill out your chart, but first look at our example on the next page:

| **Event:** I was at the DMV for over an hour, and I still couldn't register my car. |
| **Feelings:** Anger, shame, frustration |

Negative Thoughts	Mental Deception	How true? Then/Now	Alternative Positive Thoughts	How true?	How do I feel now?
"I shouldn't have to wait in line for over an hour!"	Should Statement	Then: 99% true Now: 10% true	"It was inconvenient to wait in line for such a long time, but it's not the end of the world. In fact, I actually had the rare opportunity to read my book and daydream."	100%	Much better
"People should be capable of providing me with correct information."	Should Statement	Then: 100% Now: 20%	"Nobody's perfect. I forgive the rep. for giving me the wrong information."	90%	Happy
"The representative on the phone probably gave me bad information on purpose."	Mind Reading	Then: 70% Now: 5%	"I'm sure she didn't mean to steer me in the wrong direction. Everyone makes mistakes!"	95%	Relieved
"Since my husband has a less demanding schedule, he should go to the DMV instead."	Should Statement	Then: 100% Now: 5%	"I'm glad my husband didn't have to do this today. He's had a rough week."	100%	Proud
"This has ruined my entire day."	Overgeneralization	Then: 75% Now: 0%	"Things didn't work out the way I wanted today, but life is still good."	100%	Content

NOTE: When difficult situations throw us for a loop and we're emotionally charged, they often seem **THIS** big, when in reality they are really **very small**. Tracking our mood, thoughts, and feelings and then throwing some positive statements into the mix is an effective way to put undesirable situations into perspective. Sure, your car might not be registered, but it's not the end of the world! Okay, now, fill out your own mood log below and, if you wish, continue to track your mood using the pages in the back of the book.

Event:

Feelings:

Negative Thoughts	Mental Deception	How true? Then/Now	Alternative Positive Thoughts	How true?	How do I feel now?

How did you do? Were you able to complete the chart without too much trouble? We hope so. But we wouldn't be surprised if you got stuck on the column labeled "Alternative Positive Thoughts." No, we're not doubting your intelligence—we just know how difficult it can be to find that silver lining, or to focus on that silver lining instead of the bad stuff. Sometimes, every little thing that goes wrong can feel astronomical. And we have to deliberately shrink those things down in size and impact, so they don't become harmful and contribute to depression—which is where alternative positive thoughts come in handy. Alternative thoughts put the world into perspective again; they help us step back, look at life as a whole, and recognize those small missteps as, well, small missteps.

Now, some of the best alternative positive thoughts are objective realities: statements you can't disagree with, even during the "worst of times." For example: "I live in New York City, and I love it here," or, "I'm fortunate to be in good health," or even more simply, "I'm lucky to be alive!" These may seem like cop-outs, but they're not. They're undeniable truths, and there's no reason you shouldn't use them to your benefit. In fact, you should carry them around with you every single day! Keep them on a mental list or, better yet, jot them down on a sticky note (real or virtual) and have 'em around for whenever you need them. Let's write down a few ideas on the next page:

- **I'm fortunate to be in good health.** _____
- **I'm lucky to be alive!** _____

- _____

- _____

- _____

- _____

- _____

If you're having trouble with this, think about what you might say to a friend who's feeling down. How would you comfort them? You could remind them how fortunate they are to have a great job, for example, or friends who love them. Remember, these undeniable truths are designed to put the world into a very real perspective again; to help you overcome a negatively skewed version of reality, and in turn, defeat thoughts that can lead to or contribute to depression.

◊ **To read about the symptoms of major depression, flip to the next chapter**

◊ **To gain a new appreciation for your friends and family, turn to page 93**

◊ **If you're feeling depressed in the winter, check out page 123**

◊ **To learn about antidepressants, turn to page 171**

4

Major Depression

Major depression is typically what comes to mind when people hear or read about depression. With major depression, you might be unable to fall asleep, or you might find yourself going to bed right after dinner. You might skip meals, or you might overeat. You can lose interest in sex or crave it addictively. You might get headaches or stomachaches, feel constantly fatigued (even after getting 10+ hours of sleep), forget things, or find it hard to concentrate. One thing, however, is for certain: you feel intense emotional pain.

On the next page are the criteria for a major depression diagnosis, as set forth by the American Psychiatric Association (APA). In future chapters, we'll list the diagnostic criteria for other forms of depression, too!

Criteria for Major Depression: Check Your Symptoms

The diagnosis of major depression is typically based on a person's self-report of symptoms. One must experience at least five of the following, most of the day, nearly every day, for longer than two weeks. Furthermore, the symptoms must be so severe an individual suffers personally or professionally. Check your symptoms with those below:

> ➢ Feelings of intense sadness, hopelessness, despair, or emptiness
> ➢ Loss of pleasure in most daily activities
> ➢ Significant weight gain or loss (5% or more in one month); changes in appetite
> ➢ Disruption of sleep patterns: insomnia or hypersomnia
> ➢ Changes in activity levels
> ➢ Fatigue or loss of energy
> ➢ Feelings of worthlessness, guilt, or self-hatred
> ➢ Diminished ability to think or concentrate
> ➢ Suicidal thoughts

Untreated, major depressive disorder usually lasts from six to eight months, but it can be shorter or longer and may recur. Fortunately, you don't have to go untreated–in fact, it's incredibly important that you seek treatment as soon as possible so that you can start managing your symptoms. That said, if you have a depression that feels severe and you're thinking about suicide, you should go to the hospital imme-diately. There are also people who can help you at the Na-tional Suicide Prevention Lifeline: just call **1-800-273-8255.** Someone will answer your call no matter what day or time it is.

There are several treatment methods for depression, like counseling and antidepressants, which have been proven to help many others just like you. In the meantime—say your first counseling session is coming up, or you're waiting to see a psychiatrist—you can take matters into your own hands. And you're clearly already doing that because of what's *actually* in your hands right now: this book. As we'll continue to discuss throughout the remaining chapters, you aren't pow-erless in your battle against depression. And your decision to pick up this book is just the start.

◊ To read about celebrity run-ins with depression, flip to the next page

◊ To learn about the criteria for minor depression, turn to page 37

◊ To read about how your Netflix addiction can get you in trouble, go to page 97

◊ To learn about S.M.A.R.T. goal-setting, turn to page 139

5

Celebrities Have Feelings, Too

Depression: the 6th grade bully who's acting out to feel important; the sour old man who lives next door; your happy-go-lucky coworker who always has a smile on her face.

Anybody can suffer from depression. Even the celebrities who grace our TV screens and favorite Spotify stations can struggle. In fact, creative individuals who become actors, writers, singers, and artists may be more prone to experiencing feelings of depression. Neuroscientist Nancy C. Andreasen discusses this concept in her book *The Creative Brain: The Science of Genius*. She says that creative types perceive things in a "fresh" and "novel" way, which benefits their art but also means their minds are more complex. As Andreasen explains, creative people are always asking questions that don't have easy answers, while less creative people settle in *without* question.[2]

---

2   Andreasen, N. C. (2006). The creative brain. Plume.

Fortunately for us, a growing number of celebrities choose to step into the spotlight and share their struggles with mental illness. And in doing so, they help us normalize and navigate our own mental health journeys. Below, you will find a list of celebrities who have dealt with depression, who tell their tales to help you through your journey, too:

Jim Carrey

A hysterical comedian, beloved actor, glorified icon. Jim Carrey first opened up about his battle with depression in 2004 to *CBS News*: **"There are peaks, there are valleys. But they're all kind of carved and smoothed out, and it feels like a low level of despair you live in."**[3] Carrey, while perhaps prone to depression, has learned to master his feelings. "Now, when the rain comes, it rains, but it doesn't stay," he told *iNews* in 2017.[4]

Kristen Bell

Kristen Bell's bubbly personality and infectious smile entertain, but they don't always speak her truth. Bell has struggled with depression since high school and has ad-

---

3   Leung, R. (2004, November 18). Carrey: 'Life is too beautiful'. CBS News. Retrieved from
    https://www.cbsnews.com/news/carrey-life-is-too-beautiful/
4   Aftab, K. (2017, November 3). Jim Carrey: 'People have come at me and tried to break off a piece of the Holy Grail for themselves.' iNews. Retrieved from
    https://inews.co.uk/essentials/jim-carrey-andy-and-jim-netflix/

mitted that she can lose touch with that bubbly, smiley girl on TV. **"For me, depression is not sadness. It's not having a bad day and needing a hug,"** she wrote in a very candid piece for *TIME* magazine. **"It gave me a complete and utter sense of isolation and loneliness. Its debilitation was all-consuming, and it shut down my mental circuit board."** However, Bell has since gotten help and has made it her mission to help others struggling with the illness. "It's important for me to be candid about this so people in a similar situation can realize that they are *not* worthless and that they do have something to offer. We all do," she wrote.[5]

Wayne Brady

I (it's Taylor) grew up watching and laughing at Wayne Brady on *Whose Line is it Anyway?* And I actually got to meet him about five years ago during a trip to New York City. I always thought that nothing could get this guy down—I mean, he was always smiling—but then he opened up about his battle with depression in 2014. Brady had been struggling with the illness, but realized he needed help when he broke down on his 42nd birthday. Now, he speaks out about his experience in hopes of helping others. **"I talked about it (because) I know not everyone is**

---

5   Bell, K. (2016, May 31). Kristen Bell: I'm over staying silent about depression. TIME. Retrieved from http://time.com/4352130/kristen-bell-frozen-depression-anxiety/

lucky enough to have a support system to talk to, and you may have a wall up that stands between you and help," he wrote in a tweet. "It may be pride, cultural stigma, shame, or just plain old 'I've got this!' I've had all of the above! If me talking about my personal journey helps someone, it's all worth it."

Jon Hamm

Jon Hamm, another notable actor, best known for his role in *Mad Men*, didn't always live a star-studded life. His childhood was particularly difficult, as he lost his mother at the age of 10 and his father 10 years later. He told *The Observer* that these tough losses sent him into a downward tailspin and chronic depression.[6] **"I was in bad shape. I knew I had to get back in school and back in some kind of structured environment, and… continue,"** he said. He went on to say that both therapy and antidepressants helped him manage his depression.

Ellen DeGeneres

Ellen DeGeneres is the bright light of Hollywood. She dedicates much of her time to helping those in need, rewarding do-gooders, and entertaining all of us in the pro-

---

6   Mad Men: Jon Hamm on life as Don Draper and the blessings of late fame. The Guardian. Retrieved from https://www.theguardian.com/tv-and-radio/2010/sep/19/jon-hamm-mad-men-don-draper

cess—but she's no stranger to darkness. When DeGeneres came out in an issue of *TIME* magazine back in 1997, the entertainment industry was less than supportive. She lost her television show, along with other professional opportunities, and as a result, fell into a deep depression. Fortunately, however, she sought the help that she needed and continues to live her truth while helping whomever she can along the way. **"I can't believe I came back from that point. I can't believe where my life is now,"** she told *Good Housekeeping.*[7]

Often, we view celebrities as perfect or having all they could ever want and more. In reality, they struggle too—even with depression. Fortunately, the celebrities above (and others) use their platform to speak out about their experience with depression and offer new hope when it comes to overcoming depression.

◊ **To take a depression symptom quiz, flip to the next page**

◊ **To learn about the healing power of counseling, go to page 109**

◊ **If you recently lost a loved one, turn to page 131**

---

7   Bried, E. (2017, August 10). Ellen DeGeneres' 9 secrets for living a happier life. Good Housekeeping. Retrieved from https://www.goodhousekeeping.com/life/entertainment/a45504/ellen-degeneres-cover-story

6

Your Depression Symptom Quiz

Depression symptoms can vary, depending on your depression type and severity. But common symptoms, which also make up the diagnostic criteria for major depression (discussed more extensively in chapter 4) are…

- Feelings of intense sadness, despair, and/or emptiness

- Loss of pleasure in activities you used to enjoy

- Significant weight gain or loss (5% or more in one month); changes in appetite

- Sleep disruption, such as insomnia or hypersomnia

- Changes in activity levels

- Fatigue or lack of energy

- Feelings of worthlessness or shame

- Diminished ability to think straight

- Suicidal thoughts

We've taken these symptoms and created a depression symptom quiz, designed to help you evaluate symptoms you might be experiencing. This quiz is NOT a medical or diagnostic tool. It cannot diagnose a mental health disorder. If you haven't already, go see your doctor or set up an appointment with a mental health professional. Not only can they offer you important information specific to you and the way you're feeling, but they'll work with you to determine the best treatment plan moving forward.

Now, using the chart below as a guide, rate how true each of the 15 statements are that follow on the next page. If you aren't exactly sure of your answer, or you're teetering between numbers, just go with your best guess!

Not at all	**0**
Some of the time	**1**
A good bit of the time	**2**
Most or all of the time	**3**

1. I feel unhappy and sometimes even miserable.	
2. My future isn't looking too bright.	
3. I don't feel like I have much to offer.	
4. I toss and turn in my sleep at night.	
5. I have a hard time sleeping in general.	
6. When comparing myself to others, I feel less than.	
7. I'm very self-critical and often take on blame.	
8. I've lost interest in things that used to make me happy.	
9. I'm more indecisive than normal.	
10. I feel out of touch with my closest friends and family.	
11. I have to really push myself to get anything done.	
12. My appetite/eating habits have changed for the worse.	
13. I feel tired even after I get a good amount of sleep.	
14. My life is looking and feeling pretty empty.	
15. Sometimes I think the world would be better off without me.	

Total Score:_____

After you've answered the 15 statements and tallied your score, refer to the chart on the next page to finish out the quiz and get a better idea of how severe your depression might be:

Score	Severity of Depression
0-5	Likely not depressed
6-10	Slightly depressed
11-20	Mildly depressed
21-30	Moderately depressed
31-45	Majorly depressed

NOTE: You can find 10 depression quizzes at the back of this book. Complete one each week, and make sure you write the date/time, so you can keep track of your depression symptoms over time.

◊ **For a healthy new perspective, turn to the next page**

◊ **To understand how your thoughts shape your reality, go to page 11**

◊ **If you're feeling depressed in the winter, check out page 123**

◊ **If you need a break and could use a pity party (that's okay!), flip to page 201**

7

The Best Friend Test

We're our own worst critics. We hold ourselves to impossible standards of perfection, and we come down hard on ourselves when we inevitably fall short. Fortunately, there are a few tricks that'll help. And this short chapter focuses on one: the Best Friend Test. This test is an easy way to determine whether you are being too hard on yourself.

Here's how it works: When you notice that you're judging yourself in a harsh or negative way (e.g., "I'm no good because I didn't get the job," or, "Nobody will ever want to date me,") ask yourself:

If my best friend was in the same situation as me, saying the same thing about him/herself, would I agree?

Would you tell your friend that their harsh perspective is right? Or would you tell your friend that they are being entirely too hard on him or herself? Ninety-nine times out of 100, the answer will be the latter.

The next time you suspect you're being too hard on yourself—even just a *little*—put it to the test. If you complete the Best Friend Test and still feel unsure about yourself, don't freak out. All hope is not lost. As we mentioned earlier, there are other tricks for identifying and counteracting those mental deceptions. Keep reading.

- ◊ **To read about minor depression, flip to the next page**

- ◊ **To see what celebrities have to say about depression, turn to page 25**

- ◊ **To learn another trick for thinking more rationally, go to page 113**

- ◊ **If you know something's up, but you're unsure what, find page 189**

8

Minor Depression

Minor depression is the lesser of two evils, or in other words, a milder form of depression. Now, that isn't to say minor depression is not scary and damaging—people who suffer with this disorder remain in a depressed mood for most of the day, more days than not. In addition, they present at least two (but less than five) of the symptoms listed as criteria in chapter 4 for major depression. A few of these symptoms include loss of energy, feelings of guilt, and significant changes in appetite. You can find the criteria for minor depression on the next page:

Criteria for Minor Depression: Check Your Symptoms

One must have **at least two, but fewer than five**, depressive symptoms (one must be either depressed mood or loss of interest in daily activities) during the same two-week period:

➤ Feelings of intense sadness, hopelessness, despair, or emptiness

➤ Loss of interest in most daily activities

➤ Significant weight gain or loss (5% or more in one month); changes in appetite

➤ Disruption of sleep patterns: insomnia or hypersomnia

➤ Changes in activity levels

➤ Fatigue or loss of energy

➤ Feelings of worthlessness, guilt, or self-hatred

➤ Diminished ability to think or concentrate

➤ Suicidal thoughts

Minor depression usually strikes in early adulthood, or between the ages of 18 and 25 years—a time when many of us are going through major life changes. Think: college, big moves, career, marriage... which might hint at a common cause of minor depression. While researchers still aren't certain, major life stressors (some of which we just mentioned) likely play a significant role in the development of this form of depression.

As with other kinds of depression, you don't have to just "suck it up and deal with it." In other words, you have options. There are proactive steps you can take to work through your depression. And it's important you do, so as to prevent it from becoming dysthymia: another form of depression characterized by the same symptoms, only they persist for two years or longer. In addition to consulting a therapist and/or psychiatrist (which you can read more about in chapter 18), you should embrace the power you have to practice self-care daily, which we talk about on the very next page.

◊ To read about the importance of self-care, flip to the next page

◊ To read about breaking bad habits, turn to page 103

◊ For an in-depth look at bipolar disorder, find page 151

9

The Art of Self-Care

We're going to let you in on a few self-care techniques that are *actually* worth your time and effort. Don't flip the page before you've given these some thought (and preferably some action). We're taking the time to tell you about these because they truly can work and have the power to improve your mental health:

Mindful Meditation

There's a good reason so many people meditate nowadays: doing so taps into some serious therapeutic powers. A study from Johns Hopkins University found that mindful meditation reduced symptoms of depression by 10-20 percent.[8]

---

8   Goyal, M. (2014, March). Meditation programs for psychological stress and well-being. JAMA Internal Medicine. Retrieved from https://jamanetwork.com/journals/jamainternalmedicine/fullarticle/1809754

Take a second to reflect on that: imagine feeling 10-20% happier. Sure, it's not perfect, but it's a huge improvement and without a whole lot of cost, as this practice is fairly simple. It's all about redirecting the mind and finding peace. Through mindful meditation, you learn to focus on something neutral like your breathing—in and out, in and out—and to acknowledge and then let go of thoughts. Meditation works because it helps you re-center your mind, and you can conveniently engage in the practice anytime, anywhere. Like here and now! Let's give it a try. Take five minutes to implement these beginner steps for meditating:

1. Sit or lie down comfortably.

2. Close your eyes.

3. Breathe naturally.

4. Focus your attention on your breath.

5. Notice the way your body moves with each breath.

6. Refocus the mind if it begins to wander.

How'd it go? Those six quick steps were meant to give you a little preview. If you're really interested in giving it a go, check out the resources below:

Mindful: This is a nonprofit organization, dedicated to inspiring and instructing anybody who's interested in exploring mindfulness and its positive effects on their health. Go to mindful.org to read insightful personal stories and receive helpful advice.

<u>Calm:</u> In 2017, Apple named Calm the iPhone app of the year. This mindfulness and meditation app uses relaxing visuals, soothing sounds, and a gentle voice to help guide you through the practice and ultimately bring peace and clarity to your life.

<u>Yoga with Adriene:</u> Although this is primarily a yoga You-Tube channel, the instructor also teaches a few classes on mindfulness and meditation. Adriene is super relaxed, yet engaging, and we're confident she'll help you feel at ease in this unfamiliar realm.

<u>Headspace:</u> The Headspace app is dedicated to helping its users live mindfully through meditation. It features hundreds of themed audio sessions on topics like stress, sleep, and focus, of which are designed to help listeners find their calm.

Gratitude

Nothing in life is guaranteed. Some people don't get to eat three meals a day. Some people can't see. Some people don't have a home. Our point is that whoever you are, you have something to be grateful for. Give this some thought and then make a list of what you're grateful for. Doing so doesn't diminish the reality of what hurts. But it will remind you of all the great things in life you take for granted. Here's what Taylor's list looks like today:

- I'm grateful for my dad and his undying support.

- I'm grateful to have a job I truly love and enjoy.

- I'm grateful to have two strong legs for running.

- I'm grateful for my upcoming vacation to Ireland.

- I'm grateful for the dark chocolate brownie in my hand.

Now you try. Try it three times per week, actually, as studies suggest that this will have the greatest impact on your happiness.[9] See if it does you any good. You can make your first list of gratitudes here:

- _____

- _____

- _____

- _____

- _____

NOTE: These don't have to be major assets or accomplishments. They can be more mundane things, too (like the brownie I just snarfed down).

---

9   Emmons, R. A., & McCullough, M. E. (2003). Counting blessings versus burdens: An experimental investigation of gratitude and subjective well-being in daily life. Journal of Personality and Social Psychology. Retrieved from https://www.ncbi.nlm.nih.gov/pubmed/12585811

Companion Pet

How about getting a pet? Did you know that just petting a dog or cat for a few minutes is scientifically-proven to relieve stress and anxiety?[10] This makes getting a pet potentially very beneficial and therapeutic for people who are depressed or burdened by another health issue. Hence: therapy dogs! So, we encourage you to wander on down to the nearest shelter and play with some dogs, pet the cats, and see if you feel drawn to one. Many people have found that the small amount of care a pet requires is not only doable (even with depression) but rewarding. These animals provide unconditional love and support. They don't care if you were late to work this morning or if you skip your shower tonight. They won't hold a brief freak-out against you or judge you for crying. Instead, they'll do their best to comfort you without telling you to snap out of it or urging you to feel better. Animals are happy to just hang out and share their lives with us. Here are a couple helpful resources for finding the perfect pet for you:

Petfinder: This site allows you to find all pets available for adoption near you! You can narrow your search in on dogs, cats, or whatever your preferred pet is. This enables you to find your new best friend effectively and efficiently.

---

10   Shiloh, S., Sorek, G., & Terkel, J. (2010, May 12). Reduction of state-anxiety by petting animals in a controlled laboratory experiment. Anxiety, Stress, & Coping. Retrieved from https://www.tandfonline.com/doi/abs/10.1080/1061580031000091582

<u>Found Animals</u>: This nonprofit is dedicated to putting pets in loving homes and, like Petfinder, allows you to find adoptable animals nearby. Additionally, it offers a ton of informative resources about caring for your pet. Right now, we're seeing articles about preparing for the first few days of doggy parenthood, recognizing grumpy cat behavior, and dealing with your pup's allergies.

Volunteer Work

If you're feeling a little more adventurous, try helping out the people in your community. We know what you're thinking: "Me? I can't even take care of myself!" But trust us, you can do this. In fact, helping others gets us out of our own heads! So, start by volunteering a little bit of your time at a local charity. Maybe a homeless shelter or soup kitchen. See how this experience goes (our guess is that you'll feel awesome afterwards), and then, if it goes well, start dedicating more time to helping people in need. Doing so puts the world into perspective. It connects you in a meaningful way with others. It gives you a purpose. And studies have shown that volunteering increases overall life satisfaction and lovers depressive symptoms—which certainly doesn't hurt either.[11]

---

11 Yeung, J. W., Zhang, Z., & Kim, T. Y. (2017, July 11). Volunteering and health benefits in general adults: cumulative effects and forms. BMC Public Health. Retrieved from https://www.ncbi.nlm.nih.gov/pmc/articles/PMC5504679/

To find volunteer opportunities near you, do a quick search on VolunteerMatch.org. What's cool about this site is you can narrow the search to find opportunities in specific areas that resonate with you, such as education, health, or arts and culture. What's even COOLER is that you can find virtual opportunities too (which is super convenient when you can't work up the energy or motivation to leave the house).

Music

Ah, music. Our guess is that you won't need much convincing on the therapeutic benefits of this one. Ever driven around with the radio on and the windows down and felt instantly at ease? Or blasted music in your earbuds and felt all of your problems disappear, even if just for a moment? Yeah, music does that. Famous neurologist Dr. Oliver Sacks said it best:

> *"Music can lift us out of depression or move us to tears—it is a remedy, a tonic, orange juice for the ear."*

For some, (like many of Dr. Oliver Sacks' patients) music is even more. His famous quote continues: "It can provide access, even when no medication can, to movement, to speech, to life. For them, music is not a luxury, but a necessity." Listening to music obviously doesn't take a lot of effort or skill. Anybody can do it, sure… but you can optimize the benefits by listening to music scientifically-proven to make you happy. Researchers found that the following songs in particular provide a positive listening experience and trigger the release of dopamine, the "feel-good" neurotransmitter that makes you happy:[12]

1. "Clair de Lune" - Claude Debussy

2. "Adagio for Strings" - Samuel Barber

3. "Piano Sonata No. 17 in D Minor ("The Tempest")" - Beethoven

4. "First Breath After Coma" - Explosions in the Sky

5. "Adagio for Strings" - Tiesto's Version

Did these songs do you any good? If they did, that's awesome. But if they didn't really spark your interest then that's okay too. You know yourself best, and we're sure you can think of some other songs that you know make you happy. Jot those down below for future reference, and consider creating a mood boosting playlist:

1. _____

2. _____

3. _____

4. _____

5. _____

12 Economy, P. (2017, January 5). Science says listening to these 5 songs will make you remarkably happy. Inc. Retrieved from https://www.inc.com/peter-economy/science-says-listening-to-these-5-songs-will-make-you-really-happy.html

Physical Health

Okay, now you're probably tempted to stop reading and flip the page. But we know you won't because you made us that promise! You're probably sick of people telling you to clean up your diet or to make time for the gym. We know, we're sick of it too. But we can't not touch on this because, like it or not, your physical health has a significant impact on your mental health. While people often separate the two, they actually go hand in hand: poor physical health can create and worsen mental health issues, and poor mental health can create or worsen physical health issues. The key is to invest in both to see the best ROI (return on your investment).

We know that implementing changes to your diet and activity level is hard but easing in and taking small steps can help you accomplish this important task. Let's start with the basics:

- **Get active.** The new <u>Physical Activity Guidelines for Americans</u>, issued by the Office of Disease Prevention and Health Promotion, suggest that 150 minutes of exercise each week—or 30 minutes a day, five days a week—is the most beneficial for your mental health. Start slow if you aren't accustomed to exercising. You also don't have to go to the gym if that's not your thing. Go for a walk or a run outside, dance in your living room with a friend, or do some yoga (with Adriene).

- **Eat a balanced diet.** It's okay to munch on your not-so-healthy snacks here and there (we all have a favorite junk food), but make sure you're eating enough protein, fruits, veggies, fats, and whole grains.

- **Get a good night's sleep, every night**. You probably need at least 7 hours, but you can check with the <u>National Sleep Foundation</u> to see exactly how many hours you need each night based on your age.

We know. It feels like you aren't in control—of your mind, your body, your emotions, your life. But **you** decided to pick up this book. You. Not your depression. This proves that you aren't helpless in your battle against depression. And it doesn't stop at going to therapy every Monday or taking your meds each night before bed either. If you put some real effort into taking care of yourself—whether that means meditating, practicing gratitude, adopting a pet, volunteering, listening to some uplifting music, exercising and eating healthy, or something else entirely—then you *will* see change. It might just make a world of difference. You don't have to take our word for it. Try it.

◊ **If you think you might have postpartum depression, turn to the next page**

◊ **To read about monsters under the bed, turn to page 75**

◊ **To get to know yourself a little better, flip to page 161**

10

The Baby Blues

For many parents, bringing a child into this world is the greatest accomplishment of their lifetime. After dedicating 9 months (give or take) to the growth of their baby, seeing and hearing them cry for the first time is a precious miracle. And they care for and love him/her more than words can express. But sometimes, an unwelcome wrench is thrown into those plans: postpartum depression. Postpartum depression makes parents (most often moms) feel sad, hopeless, and guilty because they either feel a disconnect with the baby or lose the desire to care for their newborn child.

People with postpartum depression present the same symptoms as those with major depressive disorder, which include insomnia, fatigue, suicidal thoughts, and irritability. The difference is that these symptoms begin during the last trimester of pregnancy or within four weeks of childbirth. If you have postpartum depression, you might also…

- **Be unable to care for yourself or your baby**

- **Be afraid to be alone with your baby**

- Have negative feelings toward your baby

- Think about harming your baby

- Worry intensely about your baby

- Demonstrate little interest in your baby

Criteria for Postpartum Depression: Check Your Symptoms

One must experience a major depressive episode with onset in pregnancy or within four weeks of their baby's delivery. The criteria for a major depressive episode is as follows:

➢ Feelings of intense sadness, hopelessness, despair, or emptiness

➢ Loss of pleasure in most daily activities

➢ Significant weight gain or loss (5% or more in one month); changes in appetite

➢ Disruption of sleep patterns: insomnia or hypersomnia

➢ Changes in activity levels

➢ Fatigue or loss of energy

➢ Feelings of worthlessness, guilt, or self-hatred

➢ Diminished ability to think or concentrate

➢ Suicidal thoughts

While negative feelings toward one's baby are almost never acted on, they're scary and troublesome, and you should tell your doctor about them right away. That said, you must also know that this is not your fault. Many people assume that something they've done is causing them to have these feelings or struggle with postpartum depression, but that is absolutely not the case. As with many other forms of depression, no one's really sure why some women develop postpartum depression (about 10-20% of new mothers), and others don't. It's likely due to the combination of a few significant factors, such as a history with depression, sudden hormonal changes, sleep deprivation, feelings of inadequacy, a lack of support, and excessive worry/anxiety. Again, if you suspect you might have postpartum depression, reach out to your doctor. With the right help, you can and will get better.

◊ **To read about how you can heal from a breakup, turn to the next page**

◊ **To better understand which areas of your life need some work, turn to page 117**

◊ **To learn about weighing costs and benefits, turn to page 127**

◊ **If you're feeling depressed after your team lost a tough game, turn to page 145**

II

The Breakup Survival Guide

Breakups sure don't help with the whole depression thing. Actually, they can worsen or even cause the whole depression thing. Breakups suck. And the following days, weeks, or even months can be tough. You've invested yourself in a person and a relationship, and then one day, it's all gone.

This can leave you reeling. The change in routine and the new, unfamiliar life without your ex (or without a significant other in general) can be hard to accept. But it isn't impossible. While it'll likely take some time—which you know if your breakup wasn't super recent—asserting control over this new chapter of your life will get you to where you want to be. So, decide that you are in control and then kick off this new beginning with the following actions:

1. Allow yourself to grieve.

Allow yourself to grieve. Sure, it's painful, but the only way to heal is to experience those difficult emotions. Instead of distracting yourself from thinking about the breakup, let your mind go there. Take the time to understand what happened, to consider what you've learned, and to say goodbye to that piece of your life. Opening up to a friend or journaling about the breakup can help you accomplish this.

2. Take a break from the digital world.

If you live in the same town as your ex, running into them at the gym or the grocery store is possible. But you know what's more likely? Seeing them on Instagram, Facebook, and Snapchat. Every. Single. Day. Unless you take it upon yourself to take a break from the digital realm or to at least unfollow their social media accounts. We could all use a social media hiatus every now and again, so this is the perfect opportunity to log off for a bit. But if you just can't or don't want to do that then deleting them can get the job done too. Now remember: This isn't about insulting or attacking your ex, but about taking the time you need for yourself.

3. Spend time with your favorite people.

You probably feel pretty lonely right about now—but you aren't alone. There are so many other people in your life that love and care about you. And we're sure they'd be happy to help you through this tough time. So, if we haven't already convinced you to do so in another chapter, open up to your people. Call your best friend and tell her you need ice cream and pizza, pronto. Better yet, go to her and have no shame in crying in her lap. Welcome the support and also take this time to appreciate your loved ones. Now that you're single again, you can focus on tending to these relationships, in addition to spending valuable time with yourself.

4. Fill the space.

Relationships take a lot of time and effort. Now, however, you have a lot of time to spare! We know you're upset about the breakup, but do your best to look on the bright side: you have the opportunity to refocus on something else you really care about (not to mention you've gotta fill the hole—take up the physical time and mental space—somehow). So, think about what fulfills you and dedicate yourself to that. Get back into something you used to enjoy. Find a new workout community. Consider taking a class. Volunteer (which you can read about in chapter 9). Really engage with whatever you choose, and make sure you're passionate about it.

5. Do some spring cleaning.

Remember how we told you to stay off social media for a while or to at least delete all traces of your ex from social media? Well, the spring-cleaning doesn't stop there. It'll help if you get rid of any painful reminders of your ex. If your kitchen reminds you of your ex because they helped you pick out the decor, consider redecorating. If your bedroom reminds you of your ex because they got you the blanket on your bed, get a new blanket. If your living room reminds you of your ex, start moving furniture. Your place will start to feel different and have less of those "he/she-used-to-sit-right-there" memories. Whatever it takes to free yourself from those painful, unnecessary reminders, do it. Do some spring-cleaning wherever you feel some negative energy hanging around.

6. Remember everything you *didn't* like about your ex.

According to science, one of the best ways to get over an ex is to think about everything they don't have going for them. A study published in the Journal of Experimental Psychology says that mulling over the unfavorable qualities of your ex-lover—say their bad nail-biting habit or their tendency to interrupt others—will help you move on.[13] Take a few minutes to paint your ex in a negative light; recall every little thing that annoyed you and find relief in the fact that you don't have to deal with it anymore. But, don't go overboard. The research team found that this is only effective when done sparingly. If you spend too much time ruminating over your ex's downfalls, you could wind up doing more harm than good to your emotional wellbeing. So, once you've spent several minutes on this exercise, move on to our other tips for getting over a breakup.

---

13   Langeslag, S. J. E., & Sanchez, M. E. (2018). Down-regulation of love feelings after a romantic break-up: Self-report and electrophysiological data. Journal of Experimental Psychology. Retrieved from https://psycnet.apa.org/record/2017-37800-001

7. Rediscover yourself.

You should also use this time to rediscover and rebuild yourself. Go dye your hair platinum blonde or get those blue highlights you've always wanted. Go on a shopping spree and update your style. Go on an over-the-top vacation to Paris or Greece with your friends. OR—don't change or do anything drastic at all. Sometimes reinventing yourself by getting a new haircut or buying a new outfit can help you feel better after a breakup. But, if that's not you, then that's okay too. In either case, just take advantage of this time you get to yourself.

8. Welcome distractions.

Remember how we said earlier that remembering your ex's undesirable qualities can help you move on? Well, that same study says that distractions are also good. Once you've done the important work that is confronting your feelings related to your ex and the breakup, do the very opposite: Think about unrelated things that make you happy. Focus on your favorite coffee shop, the crazy plotline in the book you're reading, or the cycling class you're excited to try after work. In truth, it doesn't really matter what you distract yourself with, as long as it provokes positive thoughts.

Every so often, check in with yourself to see how you're feeling. Was today particularly hard? Do you feel better today than you did two weeks ago? Is that creeping depression retreating? Ask yourself questions of the like to see where you stand and observe your improvements. This will give you motivation on even the hardest days to keep on trucking. It's hard to notice improvements when you compare one day to the very next, but when you look back at where you were a month or even a couple weeks ago, you'll be able to say, "Wow, look at all the progress I'm making." Just keep putting one foot in front of the other and know that you'll get through this.

◊ **To read about how your feelings rule your life, turn to the next page**

◊ **To learn about major depression, flip to page 21**

◊ **To read about different approaches to happiness, turn to page 177**

12

Your Thoughts Rule Your Feelings

Welcome to another chapter about reevaluating those negative thoughts (if you don't know what we're talking about, turn to chapter 2)! We want to take a second to explain why. Why is there such a heavy focus on adjusting your thinking? Why did we dedicate so much of this book to talking about this? In a few words, addressing this problem is the key to solving a lot of our problems. Seriously, think about it: our thoughts rule our feelings. And our feelings rule our lives.

Just consider it. Imagine that your day is going just fine... until your boss asks you to prepare a presentation. Immediately, the gears start turning:

1. I've always been a horrible speaker—I'm going to blow it.

2. I'll probably forget the entire thing as soon as I stand up there.

3. Everyone will see how scared I am and think less of me.

4. This is going to go so badly.

You wallow in self-pity. You feel nervous and hopeless. You even start to feel physically ill. You excuse yourself from the office and run home to curl up on your couch. What seemed like a pretty okay day turned into the worst day you've had in a while—*all* because of your negative thoughts. Sure, maybe you aren't the best at public speaking. But ruminating over worst-case scenarios isn't going to help! Instead of resorting to the negative, try putting your very best effort into thinking more positive thoughts. For example…

1. Public speaking isn't my strong suit, but I'll give it a go.

2. If I do mess up a time or two (or three), that's alright—nobody's perfect.

3. This'll give me a chance to show my worth and solidify my position in the company.

4. If I prepare a lot, I know I'll do fine! I always seem to do better than I think I will.

With this new set of positive, adaptive thoughts, you feel okay. Actually, you feel more than okay, even excited to be given the opportunity. Sure, you weren't expecting for it to be thrown into your lap like this, but no point dwelling on it. Your boss obviously trusts you to do this, and that's something to be proud of! You'll do the best you can with the presentation and maybe even knock it out of the park.

The point is that we control how we see and think about the world around us. We choose whether we're going to have a good day or a bad day—simply based on what thoughts we bring to the forefront. Which brings us to the topic at hand: the Triple Column Technique.

The Triple Column Technique, originally created by Psychologist David Burns, is one of many exercises used to get passed negative thoughts.[14] It's simple. First, you identify the negative thought. Then, you name the specific mental deception (which we'll help you with below). And finally, you brainstorm more positive thoughts. You can do this without three columns, but visuals are always helpful:

---

14   Burns, D. D. (1990). The Feeling Good Handbook. Plume.

Negative Thought	Deception	Positive Alternative Thought

So, what kind of negative thoughts might fill the first column? Well, that all depends on you. Negative thoughts vary from person to person! For now, though, we'll use those negative thoughts we identified above: You reacted negatively when your boss asked you to give a presentation. You told yourself that you'd fail, you'd forget the entire presentation, your colleagues would make fun of you, *and* that the whole thing would go poorly. Whew, that's a lot of negative thoughts! Let's fill in some of those negatives:

Negative Thought	Deception	Positive Alternative Thought
"I'll probably forget the entire thing as soon as I stand up there."		
"Everyone knows I'm awful at this."		
"When it comes to public speaking, I'm a disaster."		
"This is going to be devastating to my career."		
"Last time I spoke publicly, I was a total disaster."		

Now, which deceptions are present in this example? If we look back at those negative thoughts, there was an assortment of deceptions! One example being fortune telling, which is where you convince yourself that things will turn out badly. Fill in the chart on the next page. If you can't remember the deceptions, flip back to the list in chapter 2.

Negative Thought	Deception	Positive Alternative Thought
"I'll probably forget the entire thing as soon as I stand up there."	Fortune telling	
"Everyone knows I'm awful at this."	Mind reading	
"When it comes to public speaking, I'm a disaster."	Labeling	
"This is going to be devastating to my career."	Catastrophizing	
"Last time I spoke publicly, I was a total disaster."	All-or-nothing thinking	

Now we're at the best part: brainstorming positive alternative thoughts. Rather than assuming everything about your presentation is going to fail (which is super unlikely), take the opposite stance: "It's going to be good!" Let's bring those thoughts to the forefront and fill them in, in the last column:

Negative Thought	Deception	Positive Alternative Thought
"I'll probably forget the entire thing as soon as I stand up there."	Fortune telling	"Of course I won't forget my presentation. And if I do mess up a time or two, that's okay."
"Everyone knows I'm awful at this."	Mind reading	"I know my stuff. This'll give me a chance to show my worth and solidify my position in the company."
"When it comes to public speaking, I'm a disaster."	Labeling	"I'm nervous about public speaking, but it's not fair to call myself a disaster."
"This is going to be devastating to my career."	Catastrophizing	"This is a small presentation in front of a few people. My career and I will be fine."
"Last time I spoke publicly, I was a total disaster."	All-or-nothing thinking	"The last time I did this was when I was in school. It was rough, but a lot of people had a hard time and I actually got a good grade."

You now have another great tool for defeating the negative thoughts that wreak havoc on our minds. Remember: Most of us engage in negative thinking every single day. Even little thoughts like, "Man, I'm stupid," and, "Ugh, I shouldn't eat so much," can be classified as negative thoughts. Write them down! And, of course, counter them with some better, positive thoughts.

◊ **To read about anxiety disorders, flip to the next page**

◊ **To read more about correcting your negative thoughts, turn to page 113**

◊ **To learn about setting and maintaining healthy boundaries, go to page 185**

13

Anxiety: Depression's Partner in Crime

What's life without the occasional anxiety? You might feel anxious when a problem arises at work or when you get into an argument with a friend—that's normal. But there's a big difference between feeling anxious or worried from time to time and suffering with a serious anxiety disorder (just like there's a difference between feeling sad and suffering with any given form of depression).

According to the Anxiety and Depression Association of America, anxiety disorders are the most common mental illness in the United States, affecting 40 million adults every single year.[15] Again, there are different kinds of anxiety disorders. There's generalized anxiety disorder (which is widespread and well-known, like major depressive disorder), but there's also social anxiety disorder, panic disorder, agoraphobia, selective mutism, and more. These disorders vary in symptoms and diagnostic criteria, but they're all rooted in that crippling anxiety or fear,

---

15   Facts & statistics. Anxiety and Depression Association of America, ADAA. Retrieved from adaa.org/about-adaa/press-room/facts-statistics.

whether it's a general feeling of dread or one that's caused by large crowds or perhaps small spaces. That being said, on the next page you'll find the criteria set forth by the American Psychiatric Association for generalized anxiety disorder, to give you a better idea of what's involved.

Criteria for Generalized Anxiety Disorder: Check Your Symptoms

➢ You experience excessive anxiety or worry more days than not, over a period of at least 6 months, about a variety of events (e.g., such as attending work or school).

➢ You find it challenging to control this excessive anxiety and worry.

➢ These worries are associated with at least three of the following symptoms:

➢ You feel restless.

➢ You tire easily.

➢ You have difficulty concentrating or staying on task.

➢ You're irritable.

➢ You experience muscle tension.

➢ You have some kind of sleep disturbance (such as difficulty staying or falling asleep).

➢ Your anxiety or symptoms cause significant distress or impairment in important areas of life (e.g., occupational or social).

➢ Your anxiety is not due to the physiological effects of a substance or another medical condition.

➢ Your anxiety cannot be attributed to another mental disorder such as obsessive-compulsive disorder or panic disorder.

The cause of anxiety isn't always clear. There are biological as well as environmental factors to consider: an individual may be genetically susceptible to anxiety, or they may develop anxiety after a bad experience. Additionally, anxiety disorders can, and often do, occur alongside other mental or physical illnesses, such as depression (surprise, surprise).

We do have good news! Like depression, anxiety disorders are also treatable. And the measures you're taking to treat your depression, such as therapy or medication like antidepressants, are potentially effective in treating your anxiety as well. Now, let's delve a little deeper into these treatment methods:

Medication

While medication isn't meant to cure anxiety disorders, it is very effective in reducing or temporarily eliminating anxiety symptoms. Choosing the right medication, dosage, and treatment plan should be based on your individual needs and medical situation, done under an expert's care. And it's important to keep in mind that you and your doctor might try several medicines before finding the one best suited to your particular needs. And that's absolutely okay. That's normal. Now, when selecting a medication, you and your doctor might discuss...

- Benefits of each medication

- Side effects of each medication

- Risks of side effects (including those based on your medical history)

- Interactions with other medicines or drugs you're taking

- Alternative medicines, vitamins, or supplements

- Out-of-pocket costs

- Dosage and length of prescription

NOTE: certain medications—such as benzodiazepines, beta blockers, and antidepressants—prove to be especially helpful for anxiety (you can read more about these in chapter 28).

Counseling

Now, on to counseling! Just as with depression, a popular and effective approach for treating anxiety is counseling (more specifically, talk therapy). In this regard, the aim is to help change negative thinking patterns that cause harmful feelings (such as anxiety), and in turn, alter how one reacts to anxiety-provoking situations. For example, a counselor or talk therapist can help a person with social phobia learn how to change that false belief that others are always watching and judging them.

You have to remember that recovery doesn't happen overnight. Response to treatments can vary, and recovery doesn't always follow a linear path. In fact, more often than not, people recover in a "two steps forward, one step back" kind-of motion. You might feel better, then a little bit worse, then better, and so on. But don't mistake this for failure. Unfortunately, when results aren't immediate, sometimes people believe they've failed at treatment—or that the treatment doesn't work for them—when, in fact, the person simply needs some more time. So, even when it's hard or you don't want to, be patient and keep working at it.

◊ **To read about the monsters under your bed, turn to the next page**

◊ **To learn about negative thinking patterns, flip back to page 11**

◊ **To learn more about how counseling helps to treat depression, go to page 109**

◊ **If you get sad around the same time of the year, every year, turn to page 123**

14

Monsters Under the Bed

If you know kids, you know that when they think there's a monster under the bed, you can't convince them otherwise by simply telling them, "There are no monsters under your bed." Consider Cameron and his frustrated parents:

"There are no monsters under your bed, Cameron, we promise."

"You're wrong!" Cameron says.

"Okay, we'll prove it," his parents respond. They pull up the bed skirt and while Cameron watches from a safe distance, they look under the bed. "We're looking, Cameron, and there are no monsters under there. We promise, come see!"

Here, Cameron's thinking to himself, "Mom, you probably *think* there are no monsters under the bed, but you're wrong! Perhaps there are no monsters in the space where you're looking, but *monsters can be sneaky*! They can hide in the dark corners, behind the legs of the bedframe, or in the creases of my blankets. Still, if you stay right next to me, I might feel safe enough to crawl a bit closer and look…"

Cameron approaches. Slowly. His eyes fixed on the dark space under the bed.

"Do you see any monsters?"

"No."

"So, do you still think there are monsters under the bed?"

"Yes."

Cameron's mom takes a deep breath. His dad starts to take the lamps off the end tables and lay them on the floor, shining light that floods the whole under-bed area. Then, Cameron's parents—rolling their eyes and chuckling to themselves—physically pull themselves under the bed.

"Okay, Cameron, we're now *under* the bed, and we've searched everywhere, there are no monsters! It's pretty great under here Cam, you should come see!"

At this point, since his parents are still alive and haven't been eaten by monsters, Cameron is starting to question his narrative: **the narrative that he created for himself through the thoughts and feelings he treated as truth.** Also, he knows fun when he hears it and being under the bed is some serious fun he's missing out on! Cameron gets close… holds his breath… and sticks his head under the bed.

And from there it continues. Cameron's parents hang out with him *under the bed*. They read him his bedtime story *under the bed*. They play games *under the bed*. Under the bed becomes not a place monsters hide, but where Hot Wheels race and iPad apps are most fun. To replace his unhelpful thoughts with helpful thoughts, Cameron needed to test and experience a new story about his world. One where under his bed wasn't a scary place, but an *awesome* place.

We all have "monsters under the bed." That is, we all have stories we tell ourselves—about ourselves and the world around us—that are unhelpful. Here's a real example: I (AJ, here) once had a client who worked up the courage to accompany a friend to what she described as a "society" party. The party was hosted at the house of an important local person. At the party, there was a small high-top cocktail table upon which a large flower arrangement stood. My client leaned on the table, the arrangement tipped over, and (in what my client described as "super slow motion") it hit the floor and shattered.

She. Was. Mortified.

Now, the hosts were more than gracious: "We're so sorry! Are you okay? We knew that was a stupid thing for us to put those flowers there."

The other guests made light of the situation, sharing their own blunder stories, and reiterating that everyone unanimously agrees the table was wobbly, and it was an accident waiting to happen (and it could have happened to any of them). But, for my client, hearing statements that she mustn't be embarrassed was like telling little Cameron, "There are no monsters under the bed." She couldn't believe them for a second, and she went home knowing that she would never put herself out there again.

She explained to me in our next session, "I knew I shouldn't try to associate with important people. I don't belong there! I truly believe that incident was God's way of punishing me, of telling me, 'Know your place, Megan! Stop trying to be someone that I haven't given you permission to be.'"

Okay, so at this point, you might be empathizing with and feeling bad for Megan—somewhat because of the embarrassing moment, but even more for the narrative she's telling herself about who she is and who she had "permission" to be. It might sound crazy that someone would hold such a harsh and difficult narrative about their place in the world. However, the truth is that Megan's experience is common. We all carry with us both helpful and unhelpful narratives about ourselves and the world around us, some of which we might not even be aware of. For example, do any of these sound familiar?

Helpful Narratives:

"With hard work, I can achieve almost anything."

"There's no point in stressing out about what I can't control."

"I can figure out solutions to most problems."

Unhelpful Narratives:

"I'm not good at small talk."

"I know I'll never be rich."

"I'm not able to lose/gain weight."

"I've tried to quit smoking. I can't."

As adults, we (probably) don't have parents who will read us bedtime stories under the bed, assuring us that there are no monsters. So, taking that disadvantage into account, how do we defeat our own unhelpful narratives; our own "monsters under the bed"?

1. **Be aware.**

   We can't fix a problem if we don't know there is one. For the first step, ask yourself: "What stories am I telling myself about me, or the world around me, that are unhelpful?" Take a few moments to think about this, and then keep this question in mind for the next few days. You might not be able to identify an unhelpful narrative until it's relevant and affecting your life. For example, Cameron didn't really think about monsters under his bed until bedtime—only then would he remember he had a problem. Now, what are your monsters? We filled in an example for you:

• <u>Most people think I'm a weirdo.</u>

• _____

• _____

2. **Test the truth.**

   Unhelpful narratives portray a world, or personhood, that is disconnected from reality. For example, with Megan, the client who felt that God was punishing her for trying to be around "important people," we spent a lot of time discussing whether the story she was telling herself was true, or a destructive lie. We started looking at the implications of the narrative, challenging its merits and truth, by breaking it down into sections:

   - **Who is important? Does God believe some people are more important than others?** Megan was very religious, and when she began to think about this question, she realized that, actually, her religion taught the opposite to be true.

   - **Why would God not want you near "important people"? Doesn't God love you and want the best for you?** Here, again, Megan's beliefs about God in general didn't sync with her destructive narrative.

   - **Is it possible this was just an unfortunate incident?** That is, are you catastrophizing (see chapter 2)?

   - **Is it possible the night, as a whole, was a good night?** Therefore, could this be "all or nothing thinking"?

   - **Is it possible the hostess is thinking, "I shouldn't host parties, I screw everything up"?** Is it possible it's someone else who should be embarrassed, not you?

3. **Rewrite your story.**

The third step is an experiential one. There's a reason that if you get thrown from a horse, your instructor will tell you to get right back on. Yes, if you ride horses long enough you might one day get thrown, but it's a rare occurrence! Your riding instructor doesn't want you to create the narrative, "If I get on that horse, he's just going to throw me off." Similarly, if you get into a car accident, get back behind the wheel as soon as (safely) possible. And if you knock over a giant glass vase at a party, get back to the party!

Megan mustered up the courage to go to another event, and then another, and then another. And of course, no embarrassing incident ever happened again. Eventually, through a lot of experience (and with a lot of courage) she was able to write a new story: "God wants good things for me, and that includes socializing with whoever I want!"

Client Case Studies

I want to share with you a couple more case stories from counseling. Names and details have been altered.

Client: Sarah

Monster: Belief that she's doomed for life because she's "socially awkward"

Sarah was a professional in her late 20s, working fulltime and also finishing a post-graduate program at Harvard. Her "monster under the bed" was that she believed she was, as she described it, a permanent member of "the socially awkward club." She reported that her whole life she had felt this way, that her interests—which included obscure indie rock bands and avoiding sorority life—made her unpopular. She had accepted this narrative years ago, and had been able to live comfortably within its boundaries as she was in a relationship that served as her primary social outlet (and because her career and school took up much of her time). Recently, however, her relationship with her boyfriend of many years ended, and Sarah found herself in a profound state of loneliness and social isolation. Her narrative, once benign, now manufactured a social anxiety that prevented her from building much-needed social relationships.

I knew that Sarah's assumptions would crumble once they were tested. However, I was left with the challenge of providing Sarah with the courage to begin trying to connect with others when she was certain she would be rejected by them. She perceived herself as socially awkward, but I perceived her as exactly the type of smart, funny, anti-establishment woman the world needs more of! Her narrative (her "monsters under the bed" story that she was telling herself) was so counter-productive to her happiness, and so far from reality, that session after session it took every ounce of my willpower not to get up from my chair, walk out into the waiting room, grab someone, pull them into our session, point to her, and say, "Hey, meet this person. Isn't she cool? She's totally cool, right?!"

I was struggling with the confines of the therapy room. I couldn't exactly take her to a social event and introduce her to people. But, I determined, using some guided imagery, there was a way to help Sarah begin to lower the emotional stakes when it came to trying to meet new people.

"Sarah, I want you to imagine walking into a party. You work up the courage to go, and upon your arrival you find out it's actually an 'I hate Sarah' conference. Everyone there is wearing pins that say, 'I hate Sarah,' and they're all standing around talking about how awful you are. Now, where I want you to get, emotionally, is to a place where you can be at that party and enjoy the punch. I want you to feel so accepting of yourself, so confident, that you can stand in that room, pour yourself a punch, and say, 'Wow! These people really hate me! These people dislike me so much that they created a club to talk about it. How fascinating!' Then, imagine taking a sip of your drink and saying, 'This is delicious punch!'"

Basically, I wanted Sarah to have the narrative, "I'd prefer if people liked me, but if they don't they can suck it." At first, the proposition felt impossible: "I could **never** do that! I'd need to get the hell out of there!" So, we visualized it. Over the next few sessions Sarah began to get more comfortable with the idea. I would reiterate to her that I really don't believe there are monsters under the bed (i.e., I don't agree that she's a member of the socially awkward club), but that even if there were monsters, those monsters couldn't hurt her.

Eventually, she began to visualize herself drinking the punch. Her thinking changed from, "That would be awful," to, "Something's really wrong with these people," to, "Seriously, I feel sorry for them!" She started to build the courage to take social chances, and she reached out to some of the girls at work. Once she began testing her narrative, it fell like so much sand through her fingers. In a matter of weeks, she went from being a wallflower to the lynchpin of her social circle.

The destructive narrative was broken. We still had some work to do. For one, we spent time processing some sadness and loss—for all the years she had held onto this negative idea about herself, that she was a social outcast, when the truth all along was that she had a unique and profound ability to build genuine relationships with lots of people.

Client: Matthew

Monster: Belief that he's "permanently defective" and incurable

Matthew, a 28-year-old MIT graduate, had been depressed for what he described as most of his life. That's to say, I'm not sure exactly how long he'd been depressed. Depressed clients are horrible at determining how long they've been feeling unwell—life feels so dark to them that they believe, "There's no way I was ever truly happy. I've probably always felt this way and just didn't realize it." Regardless, when Matt began counseling at Thriveworks he wasn't expecting it to make a difference. He had seen counselors before. However, he explained that in the past, he had never "seen it through" and this time he was willing to give it one more shot. His exact words were, "I have no choice, I don't know if I want to live anymore. I think I should give counseling an honest shot."

Matt was at serious risk. He didn't have a plan or a timeframe, but he was considering suicide. With these stakes, we put together a no-suicide contract, which is an agreement between the counselor and client where the client agrees that, while he/she is in treatment, he/she won't harm him/herself. The client must agree that if he feels he might do something to harm himself, he'll remind himself of the reasons living is worthwhile, call a trusted friend, or call for emergency services to help.

The first few sessions were difficult for both of us. Matt would arrive to the session in anguish from the depression that he was experiencing: he would describe how every day felt like a year of pain. He told me that he believed he was permanently defective as a person, as he had read research articles that concluded some people are genetically prone to being unhappy (**NOTE:** many clients with depression cite this, fearing and feeling they are the extremely rare untreatable case). Here's an example of how very depressed Matt was:

As we began a session, I asked him how his week had been.

"It was okay," Matt told me, looking away and presenting a low effect.

"Any high points?" I asked.

"Not really." he said.

"Well, what'd you do this week?" I asked.

"Uh, some friends and I went to Ireland," he said.

This is how depressed Matt was. He and some friends found a last-minute airfare deal and went on a successful adventure to Ireland! By his own account, the trip was a total success, but Matt still reported that he experienced no high points!

He was spiraling lower every day. The more that Matt felt depressed, the more he told himself he was defective, which in turn made him even more depressed. I knew then that if I was going to have a chance at helping him, I needed to help him change the destructive story he was telling himself. His story was simple: **"I'm not good enough. I don't deserve to live."**

Unfortunately, I see this all too often with people from the Harvard and MIT systems (students, professors, physicians, etc.). For some, their entire lives they've been trained to value themselves based on their achievements. The problem is, once you make it to MIT, there's yet another level you're supposed to achieve, and then another, and then another. One's life story becomes:

"I'm good enough because I got a perfect score on the SATs."

"I'm good enough because I was accepted at MIT."

"I'm good enough because I'm an Olympic athlete."

"I'm good enough because I got a job at Google."

But at some point, you hit a wall…

"I studied computers at Harvard, but I'm not Bill Gates."

"I'm a professor at MIT, but my colleague won a Nobel Prize."

"I went to the Olympics, but I didn't win."

"My old roommate was on CNN this morning. I was not."

"Dr. Oz was in my graduating class. It's a harsh comparison."

"Look at what Mark Zuckerberg did. He was a freshman when I was a senior."

"I'm not good enough. I don't deserve to live."

I proposed that Matt try on a new story: **"I'm intrinsically valuable. I don't need to do anything."** Sounds like a good change, but how can Matt begin to experience this new narrative as true? This is why the connection between counselor and client is called a "therapeutic relationship." That experience can start with me. I'd say to Matt, "I perceive you as valuable, and you don't need to perform in any way to get that from me. In fact, nothing you achieve can make me think you're more or less valuable. You get full credit just by being you." With this, Matt can begin to experience that someone else believes he's valuable, and not because they're so proud of something he's done.

In addition, the thing with destructive narratives like Matt's is they can fall apart when you shine a light on them. For example, Matt was 100 times harder on himself than he was on anyone else, so we tested his narrative using the Best Friend Test (see chapter 7). I would say to Matt, "You seem to be holding yourself to a pretty high—perhaps impossible—standard. I wonder if you would be as hard on a good friend as you are on yourself?"

His answer was, "No way. I would never treat a friend like this. I would tell my friend he is fine the way he is, and I would mean it." Of course, Matt could see his own contradiction. Then, I might up the ante.

"Interesting. How about someone you don't care about quite as much. How about me? Do you feel that I need to achieve these things for me, the person sitting across from you, to be valuable?"

"Of course not! I would never believe that. That would be horrible of me."

"But Matt, you've achieved things I could never achieve. Maybe I should consider adopting your idea that 'I'm not good enough. I don't deserve to live.'"

"No, no way! It sounds ridiculous when you put it that way."

Matt began to process the flaws in his double standard. Once Matt's internal narrative changed from the destructive "I'm not good enough" to the constructive "I'm intrinsically valuable," everything changed. He began to say amazing things in session like whether he lost his job or found a better one, whether he made a great scientific discovery or not, whether he lost or gained 15 pounds, he was still just as valuable and acceptable as a person. He said, "I realize that I'm acceptable the way I am, and if I want to try and improve something in my life, I can do that; and whether it works out or not, I'm always going to be okay."

Matt began to engage openly with others—his coworkers and friends—without fear that he would be rejected or outshined. He no longer became frustrated at work, or worried about losing his job (in fact, his performance improved, and he received a promotion).

And perhaps most importantly, when Matt first came to counseling, I asked him to fill out a depression symptom inventory. He scored in the high double-digits, meaning he registered as severely depressed (to learn more about major depressive disorder, see chapter 4). Toward the end of our sessions together, I asked him to retake the same depression test and he literally laughed out loud. He said, "I can tell you without even looking at it, the score's going to be zero. I'm not depressed at all!" Not long after that, Matt and I formally ended our counseling relationship. His improved mood was still in effect during a 6-month follow up.

Our monsters under the bed or the harmful narratives we tell ourselves can destroy us. They can keep us up at night and limit our scope of the world; they can cause us to miss out on profound experiences like the beauty of social connection; and they can convince us to second guess our abilities, preventing us from reaching our greatest potential. *Unless,* we decide to challenge and defeat them—just as Cameron, Sarah, and Matt have. When we make this decision and commitment, we can destroy the monsters and harmful narratives that contribute to depression. And we can go on to live the happy, successful life we strive for.

◊ **To read about how socializing can benefit you, continue on to the next page**

◊ **To read about practices that'll make you feel good, turn to page 41**

◊ **If you need a minute to wallow in your pity, we'll join you, just turn to page 201**

15

Rewards of a Social Life

A few years ago, (it's Taylor) I went through a messy breakup. One that left me feeling depressed and lonely and honestly pretty worthless. Fortunately, though, after a month or so of sulking around, I found the silver lining: the opportunity to rediscover my independence.

I saw my friends every now and then, but I mostly spent time alone. I found solace in grocery shopping alone, going to the gym by myself, even fixing my TV and the Wi-Fi without anyone's help (this was mind-blowing to anyone that knew me). I was on a mission to reclaim my independence and prove to the world—or maybe myself—that I didn't need anyone else.

I initially felt empowered by this new lifestyle, but I slowly dipped into another depressed and lonely state. "Why am I regressing?" I wondered. Soon enough, I realized it wasn't because I missed my ex or craved being in another relationship: it was because I had isolated myself. I missed my friends and family. I was in *need* of human connection. Upon realizing this, I started prioritizing my relationships again; I rediscovered the importance of spending time with others.

Whether or not you like to admit it, the strength of your social network has a direct effect on your wellbeing. Sure, it's nice to get an unexpected bonus at work, to enjoy a delicious gourmet meal, or to win an all-inclusive vacation—but in the long run, it's not about the money, the food, or the luxuries. Those things aren't what make people happy. Love and friendship do. Social connections are a big part of what make for a happy, meaningful life.

In fact, a meta-analysis of over 300,000 people of varying ages shows that individuals with strong social relationships live longer.[16] So what are you waiting for? Get out there and socialize! Spend time with your favorite people. If you're more introverted or you've kept to yourself since you started dealing with your depression, here are a few tips for rebuilding social connections on the next page:

1. Take it slow.

Ease into becoming more social. Consider inviting a few friends over for a small get-together, make the effort to get to know one of your coworkers better, give a stranger a compliment. These are great ways to expand your comfort zone, slowly but surely.

---

16 Holt-Lunstad, J., Smith, T.B., & Bradley, J. L. (2010, July 27). Social relationships and mortality risk: A meta-analytic review. PLOS. Retrieved from https://journals.plos.org/plosmedicine/article?id=10.1371/journal.pmed.1000316

2. Be open.

It can be difficult to start up a conversation with a stranger (or even give them a compliment like we suggested above) and sometimes even with people you know and love. But if you maintain an open and friendly demeanor, people are more likely to come to you—which means the hardest part is over. Smile, use your manners, speak confidently, and put out positive vibes.

3. Stay off your phone.

Tuning into your relationships with others is pretty impossible to do if you're glued to your phone. In fact, the moment you pick up your phone, you're essentially communicating to those around you, "You're less important to me than what's going on, on this device." So, put it off to the side or maybe even put it on airplane mode, and challenge your friends to do the same.

4. Do something interactive.

Sure, it's nice to go see a movie with your friends, but it's even better if you choose a more interactive activity. Consider something that will encourage (or at least allow) conversation and connection. A few ideas: cooking dinner together, crafting, playing darts at a bar, or maybe going on a hike.

5. Don't worry what they think.

Yeah, we know, easier said than done! But hear us out for a second. We all worry sometimes about how others perceive us: "Do they like me?" "Does my hair look alright?" "Is my outfit okay?" "Am I talking too much?" But the truth is, people couldn't really care less. Often, they're too busy worrying about what you think of them! Stop concerning yourself so much with what others think of you and just enjoy their company.

◊ **To learn about the harmful effects of binge-watching, turn the page**

◊ **To read about problematic narratives flip to page 75**

◊ **To better understand what a fulfilled life looks like, flip to page 117**

16

How Do I Get Out of This Show Hole?

I have a confession (this is AJ). I'm subscribed to Netflix, Hulu, Amazon Prime, DirecTV, Showtime, HBO, PlayStation Plus, Fortnite's Battle Pass, and Disney's streaming service (as soon as it's available). It's overkill, I'll admit, but if you're like me, you love the convenience of watching your favorite shows or movies whenever you want. Sometimes, that's when they premiere live, but more often, it's when an entire season drops on Netflix… in which case, we can binge episodes in rapid succession.

Show hole depression is not really depression, but a short-term experience of depressive symptoms you might experience after you finish all the episodes of a favorite TV series (or when your favorite TV series gets cancelled). In either case, when your beloved show comes to an end, you're left with a void, which is filled with feelings of sadness, grief, loneliness, general unhappiness, and so on.

After so many episodes of marathon-watching, or seasons of a program you enjoy as they're released over the years, we start to identify and bond with those characters. Sometimes, in long-running shows like *Game of Thrones*, we'll even watch actors/characters grow up on screen. Over time, it's like that character is a friend—us viewers become invested in their story. So, when the show comes to an end, especially for good, you might actually feel the loss of your connection with those characters.

The good news is you can solve this modern-day problem. If you're feeling down after you've finished watching a favorite show, and you think you might be experiencing a show hole, turn the following tips into actions:

1. **Start watching another show now!**

   Yes, this is a bit like drinking a beer to get over a hangover, but starting another show is a quick fix for your show hole, as it will restore those positive feelings you experienced when you watched an episode of the cancelled/finished show. A hack for ensuring you like your new show is finding one with some of the same actors or producers. If they were a part of a show you liked before, the chance of you enjoying another show they're a part of is promising.

2. **Replay.**

   The characters you love are still there. Did you ever consider you could simply replay episodes you've seen before? The best part about this is because you've seen it before, you can do other things while you're watching! You don't have to focus solely on the show but can instead get some chores done or even engage in a favorite hobby like making art, scrolling through Pinterest, or practicing some yoga.

3. **Talk to other fans.**

   As you've probably learned by now, connecting with others is always a good idea. Find some friends who also watched the show and spend time together. If you don't know anyone who shares an interest, check out online groups or communities. Every show has a following somewhere.

4. **See what the actors are up to.**

   Are they joining the cast of anything new? Have they written any books about themselves or their roles? Do they host or appear in any podcasts? Chances are, your favorite actors—who play your favorite characters—are doing something.

5. **Remind yourself that it was just a show.**

   The sadness we feel after our favorite show ends results from our investment in the show and its characters. I mean, we spent the past months or even years treating the characters and the situations they found themselves as real—but they aren't. Remind yourself that while you truly enjoyed watching the show play out, it is only that: a show. And there is much else out there deserving of your time and attention.

6. **Engage in your actual life.**

   You likely put some things on the backburner when you were watching your show. Now that it's over, you can focus your energy in the real present moment again. You can even use any inspiration from the show to get into something truly rewarding.

7. **Invest in the people that matter.**

   Those characters in your favorite TV show may have felt like friends, even family… but they're made up. The people that really matter are the ones right in front of you. Your mom and your dad who would kill for a phone call from you right now. Your coworkers who keep asking you to go to lunch with them. Start putting your energy into these relationships.

8. **Change your TV habits.**

   There's no better time to recognize that your TV-watching habits could probably use a little tweaking. We know you don't want to find yourself in another show hole when another one of your favorite shows comes to an end. So, make some much-needed adjustments to your viewing habits. Consider cutting down on your TV-watching.

9. **Talk to a counselor.**

   If your depressive symptoms hang around or worsen, don't shy away from talking to a counselor. The last thing they will do is judge you, so don't worry about that—open up about what you're feeling and why you're feeling it. They will help you out of your show hole and guide you toward a happy life again.

Many people experience attachments to a TV show: to *Game of Thrones, The Office, Grey's Anatomy*, and other favorites. While it might feel fulfilling in the moment, this causes us to disconnect from the real world, from real people, from real places, from real things going on in our lives. When the series comes to its inevitable conclusion we're ultimately left feeling very alone. That's why it's so important you practice healthy viewing habits, and when you do experience feelings that come with show hole, spend time understanding them, and make adjustments so you don't find yourself back there again.

◊ **To read about creating healthy habits, flip to the next page**

◊ **If you just split from your significant other, flip to page 55**

◊ **To read about goals that are worth setting, turn to page 139**

◊ **For an in-depth look at bipolar disorder, find page 151**

17

You Make Your Habits,
and Your Habits Make You

Hitting snooze. Brushing your teeth. Closing that drawer. Tossing dirty clothes in the laundry. Driving to work. Forgetting your lunch. Locking the door. Saying, "I'm good, how are you?"

Our guess is that you engage in at least a few of these behaviors every day—without even thinking. Because your everyday is comprised of dozens if not hundreds of these little behaviors we call habits. Now, we all know that some of our habits aren't healthy or helpful: that they're outright bad habits and sometimes we can feel pretty powerless to change them. However, with a little self-reflection and informed action you can change your habits.

Change *starts* with S.M.A.R.T. goal-setting (which is covered in chapter 24). But it doesn't stop there. It involves breaking our bad habits and building healthier ones, even when it's hard—and it's often hard. Habits are hard to change because they're automatic, but the surest way to get rid of a habit you don't like is by creating a new one. For example, if you want to stop eating potato chips every day at lunch, it'll prove beneficial to replace them with something else like nuts or carrots, as opposed to *just* cutting chips out of your diet.

It depends on the person, but researchers from University College London found that it takes an average of 66 days to cement a new behavior pattern in our minds.[17]

After that, we generally don't think about what we're doing—we just do it! So, really, building a new habit happens with one decision... one moment... one day at a time. What about you, and what about today? Take a few minutes to think about the good and bad habits in your life, which you can record here and on the next page:

Good Habits That Benefit Me:

- **Biking to work.** _____

- _____

- _____

---

17 Lally, P., Van Jaarsveld, C. H., Potts, H. W., & Wardle, J. (2010) How are habits formed: Modelling habit formation in the real world. European Journal of Social Psychology. Retrieved from http://repositorio.ispa.pt/bitstream/10400.12/3364/1/IJSP_998-1009.pdf

Bad Habits That I Want to Change:

- Spending hours a day on Instagram. And Snapchat. And Facebook.
  _____

- _____

- _____

Now to the doing! Remember: breaking bad habits isn't painless. Pain is the cost, but it comes with rewards too. Take a look to see how you can break bad habits by creating new ones:

> Holly wants to stop watching so much TV at night. So, she stays at work longer; she keeps the remote control away from her bed; she plans out the shows she will watch; and she cancels Netflix (but keeps Amazon Prime). Additionally, she invites friends over on a regular basis to hang out.

Notice what Holly did? She **(1)** identified the behavior she wanted to change, **(2)** took specific steps to make it harder to engage in the behavior (moved the controller and canceled Netflix) and **(3)** rewarded herself with a better alternative (time with friends). Now, here's an example of creating an entirely new habit:

> Daniel wants to work out more and sets the goal of going to the gym three times a week. He makes a playlist with his favorite music, lays his exercise clothes out, and sets up a

regular time to meet a buddy at the gym. He also rewards himself for working out by picking up his favorite fruit smoothie only after his workouts.

See what Daniel did? He **(1)** set a doable goal, **(2)** did everything possible to make it easier and more enjoyable (created a workout playlist, set out exercise clothes), and **(3)** rewarded himself when he did succeed (favorite fruit smoothie).

So, here's the secret: Good intentions without intentional actions are worthless. Success doesn't just happen. And you can utilize cost and reward to your benefit:

- **Creating a new habit: Decrease the cost, increase the reward**

- **Breaking a bad habit: Increase the cost, find an alternative reward**

Now, it's time for you to put this formula to the test. From the previous page, take one of the habits you want to change and apply what you've learned:

What bad habit do I want to break? _____

_____

- **How can I increase the cost?** _____

_____

- **How can I provide an alternative reward?** _____

_____

What new habit do I want to create? _____

_____

- **How can I decrease the cost?** _____

_____

- **How can I increase the reward?** _____

_____

Now you have your plan. Remember, 66 days. If you can pay attention to staying on track for 66 days, your new habit will become second nature.

- ◊ **To read all about how depression counseling can help, flip to the next page**

- ◊ **To read about how socializing can benefit you, go to page 93**

- ◊ **If you're mourning a tough loss, turn to page 131**

18

Depression Counseling

Counseling has helped millions of people live happier, healthier lives and can be extremely helpful in the treatment of depression. Counseling is your safe place. You don't have to worry about being judged or ridiculed—your only focus should be getting down to business and getting the most out of your time in session. If you haven't been to counseling before, or haven't been for a while, here are some tips to help you get the most out of your time with your counselor:

1. **Remember that your counselor is on your side.**

   Your therapist's ultimate job and goal is to help you lead a better life. They are there to guide you and support you, and they're also going to challenge you when it proves helpful to the process. It's particularly important that you remember, no matter what, your counselor is on your side.

2. **Don't keep secrets from your counselor.**

   A key to success is being open with your counselor. It makes a difference when you lie about "little, insignificant" things, like how the fight between you and your partner unfolded this morning. You might not want to tell your counselor how you blew up or that your partner ran out of the apartment crying. But you need to share difficult truths, so your therapist can best help you.

3. **Understand that it sometimes gets worse before it gets better.**

   Therapy can be hard. It often involves talking about tough subjects, revisiting the past, and confronting painful emotions. Sometimes you might even leave a session feeling worse than you did at the start of it. But that's normal—it's, at times, an essential part of the growth and healing process. Change rarely happens overnight, but it *does* happen. Keep your eye on the prize and continue working with your counselor toward your goals.

4. **Acknowledge that counseling is your time.**

   Counseling is your time to focus solely on you... which might be difficult if you aren't used to being the center of attention. But that's what counseling is all about: its sole purpose is to serve you. While it might feel embarrassing or uncomfortable at first, you'll soon get used to it. And then, you'll understand just how valuable your time in counseling truly is.

Sometimes, someone recognizes the benefits of counseling, but their nerves get the best of them. They mull the idea of counseling over and over again—they just can't bring themselves to take the leap. This hesitation is understandable, but the benefits of counseling are just too great to miss out on. So, consult these tips, and take that leap.

◊ To read about a test called the Survey Method, turn to the next page

◊ If you're struggling to connect with your newborn, flip to page 51

◊ To read about different kinds of depression, flip to page 189

◊ To read about the benefits of throwing yourself a pity party, turn to page 201

19

Employ the Survey Method

While the Best Friend Test (discussed in chapter 7) is an effective strategy for recognizing our mental deceptions, sometimes we need additional evidence. Or a plan B, at the very least. In either case, the Survey Method comes in handy. It's simple. Whenever you're in need of another perspective or more information, ask yourself this:

Would other people agree with this thought? Would they draw the same conclusion?

Then, rather than keep this question a hypothetical one, get out there and find the answer. Survey your friends, family, coworkers... whoever you deem fit. Like this:

Caitlin has wanted to be a teacher for as long as she can remember. In high school, she worked hard to get all A's to ensure she'd get into college and have the opportunity to turn that vision into reality. And so, she did. She got ac-

cepted into college and earned a degree in early childhood education. Today, Caitlin's living out her lifelong dream and beginning her second year of teaching kindergarteners. But she's having doubts. The past few months have been incredibly stressful and tiring. And now she wonders if she's chosen the right career path... if she's suited for the job... or if her kids deserve better.

Caitlin sees her stress and exhaustion as weaknesses and convinces herself that she's doing a disservice to her students. "Good teachers don't show up to work this stressed and tired. My kindergarteners deserve better," she tells herself. But before she makes any rash decisions, she decides to talk to a few fellow teachers about how she feels. "Do you ever feel exhausted at work? Do you wonder if you're truly cut out for the job?" she asks them. The overwhelming response is yes—which shocks Caitlin. They all share their moments of doubt, but assure her that these weak moments are fleeting... and they do not mean Caitlin isn't right for the job. In fact, she's perfect for the job, they tell her.

Caitlin used the Survey Method to gain perspective on her mental deception and ultimately realized she was being way too hard on herself. Had she not employed this trick, it's possible Caitlin would've continued to believe the harmful lies she was telling herself. See how this works? This tool can expose the harmful lies you're telling yourself, too. And, of course, ultimately aid you in your fight against depressive thoughts.

◊ To read about prioritizing every area of your life, flip to the next page

◊ To learn about effective self-care techniques (like meditation), turn to page 41

◊ If you're going through a rough breakup, turn to page 55

◊ If you've recently lost a loved one, turn to page 131

20

A 360° Life

*I'm just trying to get by. To make it 'til 5.
To make it 'til Friday. To make it 'til Spring Break.*

Ever felt like this? We know you have—we've all been there. Things pile up: Work. School. Work. Rent. Did we mention work? And too often, we focus on one area of our life, while we let the others slide. It's like that saying: First, we sacrifice our health to make money. Then, we spend all our money to try to get healthy. Ouch!

A 360° life is a life where no major aspect is neglected. As you can imagine, this kind of life supports a happy, healthy mind and, therefore, can seriously assist your fight against depression. So, how can you get there? On the next page, there is a 360° Life Chart, which features eight sections: work/career, finances, health, family and friends, romance, personal growth (which includes spirituality and creativity), fun and recreation, and physical environment. This concept, originally called the Wheel of Life, was created by Paul J. Meyer, founder of Success Motivation Institute, Inc. He promoted it as a tool for finding balance, happiness, and success in life.[18]

Take a minute to look at the 360° Life Chart on the next page and think about your satisfaction on a scale of 1-10 with each area of your life. Remember, you're rating *your* satisfaction—not what society or anyone else says is a 10. For example, you don't need to be a millionaire to score a 10 in finance. You don't need to live in Buckingham Palace to score a 10 in physical environment.

360° Life Chart

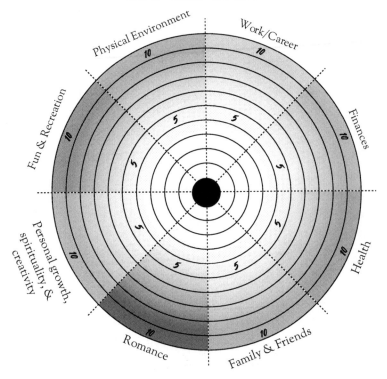

---

18   The Wheel of Life: Finding Balance in Your Life. Retrieved from https://www.mindtools.com/pages/article/newHTE_93.htm

Where do you rate your life fulfillment in each category? Rate them on a scale of 1 (very unsatisfied) to 10 (very satisfied), by coloring in your own 360° Life Chart below. Then, make a personal note about each category. For example, I rate my environment a 7. My personal note would read: "I love living close to downtown, but I'd like to spend more time outside." Now, it's your turn:

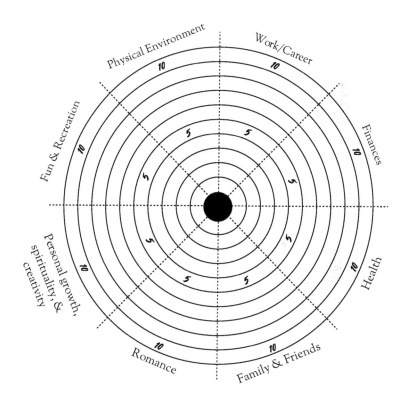

1. Environment

Personal Note: _____

_____

2. Work/Career

Personal Note: _____

_____

3. Fun & Recreation

Personal Note: _____

_____

4. Romance

Personal Note: _____

_____

5. Personal Growth, Spirituality, & Creativity

Personal Note: _____

_____

6. Finances

Personal Note: _____

_____

7. Health

Personal Note: _____

_____

8. Friends and Family

Personal Note: _____

_____

Let's say you rated your "Friends and Family" category a 4 and noted that you haven't spent meaningful time with your friends in a few weeks. You've identified a problem—one that you can address. And when you address it, you'll improve your overall life satisfaction in the process.

Now, you have a pretty good idea of where you're thriving and where you could improve. Sure, it might feel funny to rate your life in this way, but self-reflection and self-aware-ness are important. Change is a process—it doesn't happen all at once. It involves this self-reflection and thinking about what is most important to *you*, your health, and your happiness.

◊ To learn about depression in the winter, turn to the next page

◊ To read about the lies we tell ourselves every single day, turn to page 11

◊ If you're looking to get to know yourself a little better, turn to page 161

21

Winter Depression

A lot of things can bring on bouts of depression: a messy breakup, a loved one's passing... or even changes in the weather. It might sound silly to those who haven't experienced it themselves, but the weather can bring on depression—or more specifically, the cold, dreary, **dark** weather that comes with the winter months can bring on depression.

Seasonal affective disorder (SAD) is a form of depression that's rooted in these seasonal changes. In the majority of cases, individuals start to experience symptoms in the fall, which continue and/or worsen throughout the winter months (although it is possible to experience SAD in other seasons). The exact cause of this type of depression isn't certain, but many speculate that it has to do with light exposure, or lack thereof. The findings of a four-week study support this theory: Researchers assigned 96 patients with SAD to one of three light treatments. These patients either got an hour and a half of bright light exposure in the morning, an hour and a half of bright light exposure in the evening, or a placebo.

After several weeks, more patients in the morning light and evening light groups experienced a greater reduction in symptoms than those in the placebo group. This study, as well as many others that have followed, suggest that lower exposure to light can contribute to depression and bright light treatment can help.[19] Now, on the next page, you'll find criteria for SAD:

---

19   Eastman C. I., Young, M. A., Fogg, L. F., et al (1998, October). Bright Light Treatment of Winter Depression. JAMA. Retrieved from https://jamanet-work.com/journals/jamapsychiatry/fullarticle/204290

Criteria for Seasonal Affective Disorder: Check Your Symptoms

One must present a pattern of winter depression for at least two winters (back to back), and it must be severe enough to meet the criteria of major depressive disorder. To do so, one must experience at least five depressive symptoms, most of the day, nearly every day, for longer than two weeks—and they must be so severe the individual suffers personally and/or professionally. These symptoms include:

➤ Feelings of intense sadness, hopelessness, despair, or emptiness

➤ Loss of pleasure in most daily activities

➤ Significant weight gain or loss (5% or more in one month); changes in appetite

➤ Disruption of sleep patterns: insomnia or hypersomnia

➤ Changes in activity levels

➤ Fatigue or loss of energy

➤ Feelings of worthlessness, guilt, or self-hatred

➤ Diminished ability to think or concentrate

➤ Suicidal thoughts

According to Mental Health America, about 5% of the U.S. population experiences seasonal depression in any given year.[20] This might get you to thinking: "Do I have SAD?" But a better question to ask yourself is, "Do I feel depressed in the winter?" If the answer is yes, compare your depressive symptoms with those listed in the chart above. And if signs point to you having this disorder, talk to a mental health professional about your concerns.

One last thing: do what you can to take extra good care of yourself in the winter months. This can involve engaging in the self-care activities we discuss in chapter 9, as well as talking with your doctor about trying a light therapy lamp.

◊ **To read about the costs and gains involved in goal-setting, flip to the next page**

◊ **To gain a new appreciation for your friends and family, turn to page 93**

◊ **To better understand how your everyday habits affect you, turn to page 103**

20 Seasonal depression. Mental Health America. Retrieved from http://www.mentalhealthamerica.net/conditions/sad

22

The Price Is Right... Or Is It?

When you think about the word "change" what thoughts or emotions come to mind? Most of us desire change in some way. We want to become better people; we want to be happier. But we also often come up short of making changes. Why? Because change isn't ~~always~~ *usually* easy. There's always a cost. Saying "yes" to one thing means saying "no" to something else:

- I want to be healthier... but I also want to eat these Doritos.

- I want to save money... but I also want to backpack across Europe.

- I want to spend more time with my friends... but I also want to go home.

Get the gist? Every choice has a price. It's helpful to weigh costs and benefits, then decide: Is it worth it?

In the following exercise, identify three goals (look at chapter 24 to understand how to create S.M.A.R.T. goals) and analyze the costs and the gains for each. Ask yourself, "Am I really willing to pay the price?" We completed an example for you to look at first:

Goal: Read a new book every month.

What are the costs? I'll have to cut back on some of the other things I like to do like surfing Reddit, watching Netflix, etc.

What are the gains? I'll read at least 12 books a year and benefit from the satisfaction of replacing TV time with book time.

Am I willing to pay the price? ⟨Yes⟩/ No / Unsure

Goal 1: _____

What are the costs? _____

_____

What are the gains? _____

_____

Am I willing to pay the price? Yes / No / Unsure

Goal 2: _____

What are the costs? _____

_____

What are the gains? _____

_____

Am I willing to pay the price? Yes / No / Unsure

Goal 3: _____

What are the costs? _____

_____

What are the gains? _____

_____

Am I willing to pay the price? Yes / No / Unsure

NOTE: This exercise isn't meant to discourage you from setting goals or making commitments. Instead, it's supposed to help you gauge whether or not those goals or commitments are best for you right now! Because the reality is that sometimes the costs just aren't worth it. At least not at this point in time.

Let's talk about snowboarding. The costs of learning to snowboard are brutal! Much worse than learning to ski. Be prepared to fall. Hard. A lot. Here's the thing—most people who try to learn to snowboard give up midway. After a lot of falling and pain, they decide the costs are too great. What a waste! It's a fine decision to learn to snowboard. And it's a fine decision to take the less brutal route and ski instead! What doesn't make sense is forging ahead without weighing the costs. You might find yourself bruised and broken and still not able to snowboard! This is a lose-lose situation. So, weigh the costs and *then* make your choice.

◊ **If you're grieving the loss of a loved one, flip to the next page**

◊ **To read about different kinds of bipolar disorder, turn to page 151**

◊ **To learn about antidepressants, find page 171**

23

Grief and Depression

Sometimes, life really sucks. You lose your job of 10 years, a relationship of 8, or a loved one dies. And you can't just buckle down and then move on—instead, you're overwhelmed with grief: an intense, paralyzing, dark feeling.

The feelings of depression and grief often blur together. While the latter can lead to the former, there is a difference between grieving and being clinically depressed. Here's the difference: grief (or bereavement) is a normal human response to a significant personal loss. One is typically not diagnosed with clinical depression unless the symptoms last for more than six months. Now, your grieving process might look like some combination of the following:

Denial and Seclusion

This isn't happening. This can't be happening…

No one wants to believe their sister has died. Similarly, no one wants to hear they're being let go from the job they've dedicated the last 15 years to. Instead, we reject the truth of the matter and do our best to avoid the devastating feelings that come with such a loss. It's our instinct to react this way, to try to protect ourselves temporarily from the pain.

Anger

How could you do this to me?
How could you leave me?

It's also common to react with the intense emotion of anger. Many people view anger as a negative emotion, one we should avoid. But that's not really the case. Anger is an important emotion to experience and express. It's our natural response to a perceived injustice. So, while you might, out of habit, work to cover up your angry feelings, don't. It's important you acknowledge your anger—as it's an expression of the love you feel for the person or thing that you've lost.

Bargaining

If only I'd been there to help.
If only I'd said I love you more often.

This stage is all about guilt. Instead of accepting what is, the individual thinks about how they could have helped; what they "should" have done differently. For example, if someone's pet passes away sooner than expected, the owner may wonder how they could/should have cared for the pet differently. Bargaining is ultimately a way of telling ourselves that we're in control of our world around us (which, of course, we are not).

Depression

I can't get out of bed. There's no way I'm pretending like
everything's okay.

This is the part where you're overwhelmed with feelings of sadness and despair, which often overshadow everything else in your life (we're sure this sounds familiar). It might be smart to spend some time reflecting inward and working through these feelings. However, it's also important that you lean on others for support when you need it, so that any depressive feelings you're experiencing don't find a permanent home.

Acceptance

I miss you, and I hate that you're gone. But I have to carry on.

Then, there's the stage of acceptance. This is the stage where the grieving individual is able to acknowledge what has happened and finally find some sort of peace. Once you've reached this point in the grieving process, you're typically able to move on and you're no longer at a great risk of falling into a serious depression. One of my clients (AJ, here) went through an abrupt and painful breakup (10 out of 10 on the pain scale). This client went through all the stages of grief—at the beginning, he was crying a lot, he could barely function.

What's really amazing is one day, after a number of weeks, he came in and said, "Today I woke up, and it felt like the ton of bricks I've been carrying on my shoulders had fallen off. I did a quick check and noticed that for the first time in a long time, I don't feel any pain. I feel great. Life feels bright again." That's acceptance, and it's miraculous.

These are the five universal stages of grief: denial, anger, bargaining, depression, and acceptance. They were first proposed by Psychiatrist Elisabeth Kubler-Ross in 1969 and have since been widely used to describe how we react to heartbreaking losses.[21] But here's the thing: coping with a difficult loss is ultimately an incredibly individual and personal experience. You might progress through these stages as described above, you might experience these stages in a *different* order, or you might even go through some of them more than once. But in any case, a tough loss often changes life as we know it:

You used to love waking up for your early morning run. Now, you're lucky if you climb out from under the covers before noon.

You've always been a social butterfly. But now, you have no desire to be around anyone. You wish everyone would just leave you alone.

You can't find a reason to feel happy. Rarely do you crack a smile or let out a laugh. It feels fake if you do.

A difficult loss can lead you into dangerous territory. Fortunately, though, you can take action to prevent your grief from progressing into depression. Here are a few guidelines that might help you out:

---

21   Gregory, C. (2019, April 11). The Five Stages of Grief. PSYCOM. Retrieved from https://www.psycom.net/depression.central.grief.html

1. Feel.

Give yourself permission to feel your emotions. Don't try to avoid, minimize, or refute your feelings (no matter how tough they may be to endure). Instead, welcome them. We know how incredibly hard this is, but you need to first acknowledge your feelings so you can then begin to process them and work your way through them.

2. Don't shy away from support.

Lean on your loved ones. Don't shy away from their support, and don't think of yourself as a burden. Find the courage to tell your friends you could really use someone to talk to (and a pint of chocolate chip cookie dough on the side). And then watch as all of the support comes flooding in.

3. Seek professional help.

Pay attention to when your loved ones *can't* give you the help that you need. Don't hesitate to get professional help if you think you need it or if you think you might benefit even the slightest from it. People are often surprised by how helpful sessions with a skilled licensed counselor or psychologist can be. You can read more about the benefits in chapter 18.

Grief can strike without a moment's notice—and it often does. If you're suffering as the result of a difficult loss, don't ignore your feelings. Work through them. Reach out to your loved ones for support. And please, don't be afraid to seek professional help.

◊ To learn about smart goal-setting, flip to the next page

◊ To learn about the symptoms of anxiety, turn to page 69

◊ If you need help correcting your negative thinking patterns, turn to page 113

◊ To read about why setting boundaries is important, turn to page 185

24

How to Set a Goal

Contrary to popular belief, January is not the only time to set and work toward your goals. Happy, successful people are setting, revising, and achieving goals all the time. Goals motivate you, keep you accountable, give you purpose, and ultimately help you live your best life.

We want to help you learn to set goals that yield real results, or **S.M.A.R.T. goals**.[22] In other words, to set goals that are Specific, Measurable, Attainable, Relevant, and Time-bound. Here are clear instructions for doing so:

Specific: Your goal should be clear and unambiguous. You should be able to identify exactly what is expected and define the 5 W's. In this case: who, what, which, where, why.

- Who: Who is involved?

- What: What do I want to accomplish?

---

22 Doran, G., Miller, A., & Cunningham, J. (1981, November). There's a S.M.A.R.T. way to write management's goals and objectives. Management Review.

- <u>Which:</u> Which requirements and constraints do I need to be aware of?

- <u>Where:</u> Where will my goal happen?

- <u>Why:</u> Why do I want to do this?

Measurable: How will you measure progress toward reaching this goal? The thought behind this is that if a goal is not measurable, it's not possible to know whether you're making progress. You should be able to answer questions like:

- How much?

- How many?

- How will I know when I have accomplished my goal?

Attainable: Ensure that your goal is realistic and achievable. It should neither be out of reach nor too easy, as the latter is pretty much meaningless. An attainable goal will usually answer the following questions:

- How can my goal be accomplished?

- Do I have, or can I get, what I need to achieve the goal?

Relevant: This stresses the importance of choosing goals that matter. Think about how this goal fits into the grand scheme of things. Why is it worth doing? Is it worth the cost (see chapter 22)? Does it line up with your vision? Your mission? A relevant goal will motivate you and enable you to answer "yes" to these questions:

- Is this worth the cost to me?

- Am I willing to pursue, and complete, this goal now?

- Does pursuing and achieving this goal make sense for my life?

Time-bound: And finally, be specific in how much time you want to commit to this goal and when you want to reach it. A commitment to a deadline helps you to focus your efforts on completion and prevents day-to-day distractions. A time-bound goal will usually answer these questions:

- When will I achieve my goal?

- Is my timeline realistic?

- What do I have to do to achieve my goal by the designated deadline?

Now, let's look at a S.M.A.R.T. goal. Is the common, "I want to get in shape," a S.M.A.R.T. goal? No, it isn't specific, measurable, or time-bound! It barely meets any of the criteria. So, what *is* an example of a S.M.A.R.T. goal? How about, "I want to lose 10 pounds in 6 weeks." This is a S.M.A.R.T. goal because it is…

Specific: You've determined a clear objective in identifying how much weight you want to lose.

Measurable: You can track your goal by weighing yourself on a scale.

Attainable: A loss of 1.67 pounds a week is realistic and attainable (for some people, not everybody, and that's okay).

Relevant: Your goal is appropriate and important (unless you're already at an ideal weight or you're underweight).

Time-bound: You've determined a time when you want to (and reasonably can) accomplish your goal.

Now, take a few minutes to stop and think: *What are three goals I want to work toward in the next six months to a year?* And, of course, make these S.M.A.R.T. goals:

1. _____

_____

2. _____

_____

3. _____

_____

Read over each goal you just wrote. If you can say, "I will be happy with my progress in life if these goals are met," then that's a promising sign that you've set excellent goals. If not, make some revisions!

Goal-setting probably isn't the first thing that comes to mind in thinking about your fight against depression. But, as we mentioned earlier, it plays an instrumental role in living a happy, fulfilled life. And when you don't feel happy or fulfilled, you're at a greater risk of suffering from many harmful symptoms of depression like feelings of worthlessness, hopelessness, and a loss of pleasure or interest in life. At the same time, finding fulfillment in your everyday can help **remedy** these symptoms of depression. So, make S.M.A.R.T. goal-setting a priority.

◊ **To read about how watching sports can make you depressed, flip the page**

◊ **To learn about all that comes with minor depression, turn to page 37**

◊ **For a list of depression types (not covered in other chapters), flip to page 189**

25

Sports Fan Depression

The first time a client came into my office (it's AJ), explaining that he was feeling depressed after his favorite hockey team had lost a playoff game, I thought he was either exaggerating or being sarcastic. But he was serious, and over the course of the hour he explained his feelings of loss, despair, irritability, anger, and his inability to focus at work (all common symptoms of depression). I thought, "What a rare and unusual case!"

Not long after the session, I was talking with another clinician at the practice, and she was telling me how she was having the same depression symptoms—in response to the same game! **It turns out that experiencing the blues after a sports-related defeat is a common experience for sports enthusiasts, and for some, the symptoms can be shockingly painful.** Are you feeling down after a sports-related loss? Here are several strategies for beating those blues:

1. Take a step back.

The networks do a great job before a game, especially a championship game, to make it sound like the most important thing that has ever happened in the history of mankind is about to go down. Of course, they never say, "…and remember, it's just a game." This, in combination with the fact that you're a huge fan of your team, makes the situation a very emotionally charged event. Here's the thing: when something is emotionally charged, it looks and feels a lot bigger than it really is. Yes, your team lost—and that sucks. But 99.9% of the things in your life are unaffected and unchanged. Taking a step back will give you a broader perspective to put this loss in its rightful place (a place that won't ruin your week).

As an exercise, try listing things in your life that aren't related to the sports team—specifically things that are going well. For the moment, ignore any areas that aren't going great (if you're feeling depressed, you'll have a tendency to focus on things that are not going well—fight this). Write down things that bring you happiness. Maybe you love your new city, you're feeling grateful for your family and friends, you really enjoy this time of year, or you're simply in good health. Give it a go on the next page—we already got you started:

- I love living in Seattle.
- I've made some really great friends this year.
- It's finally fall, and fall is my favorite.
- _____
- _____
- _____

As you "take a step back" you'll begin to see that the sports event is a small part of your life's big picture, and it doesn't need to have any power over how you feel.

2. Stay social.

People who are feeling down or depressed have a tendency to isolate themselves. Also, if the sports season is over, you might be missing that pre-scheduled time every week or few days to get together with friends to hang out and watch the game. Social withdrawal only makes one's mood worse. So, make an effort to keep your social life strong, even if you don't think you're feeling up for it.

3. Fill the void.

If you're a die-hard fan and the season is finished, you're going to notice a post-season void. Fill the mental and emotional space with something else... something else you enjoy: a project, hobby, group, or event to get involved in. Here are a few options to consider:

- Plan a camping trip.

- Have friends over for a weekly dinner tradition.

- Pick up reading or writing again.

- Join a dance class or rec. sports league.

- Start watching another sport!

In all honesty, it doesn't really matter what it is that you do. Just do something (something you enjoy, of course).

4. Talk about it.

Talking about your sports fan blues with a friend will help you to process the disappointment that you're feeling. Commiserate with other fans who are having some of the same feelings. It can help just to know that people care (and they do) and to be reminded that you're not alone. Pretty soon you'll be talking less about the loss, and more about what your team's going to do next year (they're going to crush it, of course).

5. Wait it out.

"Sports fan depression" is probably better described as the "sports fan blues." While the symptoms can mirror those of depression—and while they can be surprisingly painful and disruptive—they generally have a short half-life. In most cases, you'll feel better in a few days (to be diagnosed with something like major depressive disorder, the symptoms would need to be more longstanding; or more specifically, last at least two weeks). That said, if it has been a few days and you're not feeling better, or if your symptoms are so severe that they're affecting your sleep, work, or relationships, you might want to consider meeting with a healthcare professional like a licensed professional counselor.

The Red Sox went 86 years without winning a World Series. People lived their entire lives and didn't see a victory. But, if you're in Boston, what are you going to do? Abandon the Sox and become a New York Yankees fan? Not a chance! Remember, you never know what's going to happen. It seems that every year at least one team that's favored does awfully, and a team with low expectations has a record-breaking season. So, stick with your team and ride out those tough losses together. And when you do start to suffer after your team loses, remember the tips from this chapter.

◊ **To learn about bipolar disorder, flip to the next page**

◊ **To learn about how your beliefs create your reality, flip to page 11**

◊ **If you want to read about how a counselor could help you, turn to page 109**

◊ **To read about the importance of weighing costs and benefits, turn to page 127**

26

Bipolar I and II:
When Depression Meets Mania

"I sought and received treatment, I put positive people around me, and I got back to doing what I love—writing songs and making music."

This chapter covers some potentially confusing stuff. Confusing stuff that might actually resonate with you and leave you feeling worried or concerned. Which is why we thought it a good idea to kick the chapter off with a light-at-the-end-of-the-tunnel quote by Mariah Carey. After 17 years of struggling with bipolar disorder, Carey revealed her diagnosis to the world in April of 2018. In her big reveal to *PEOPLE*, she explained that she's doing much better today thanks to a combination of effective treatments like therapy and medication.[23]

Carey is living proof that being diagnosed with bipolar disorder is not the end of the world. You just have to address the issue and then you can get back to your life… which may or may not mean selling hit records and singing in front of thousands and thousands of people. Now, let's dive right in, shall we?

Bipolar I disorder, sometimes called manic depression, is characterized by changes in mood, from "normal" to intense states of either depression or mania. You, of course, don't need a detailed definition of depression—but if you're wondering what mania is, it's a state characterized by periods of overactivity (we'll explain more later). Now, in order for an individual to be diagnosed with bipolar I disorder, he or she must meet the diagnostic criteria for a major depressive episode, in addition to experiencing manic episodes.

What? Yeah, that was a mouthful. Like we said, this isn't the simplest stuff. But we're going to break it down for you: there are three major types of bipolar disorder and a fourth category for bipolar symptoms that don't fall under the other umbrellas. There's bipolar I, bipolar II, a third called cyclothymia, and then a fourth category for other bipolar and related disorders:

- People with **bipolar I** experience **manic episodes** in addition to depressive episodes.

- People with **bipolar II** experience *hypomanic* (lower intensity) **episodes** in addition to depressive episodes.

- People with **cyclothymia** have **hypomanic** and **depressive** *symptoms.*

- Everyone else with bipolar disorder symptoms that don't fit the criteria for the former three categories fall into the broader fourth category.

Is it starting to make a little more sense? Let's break these down even further:

Bipolar Type	Definition	Episode Type	Additional Notes
Bipolar I Disorder	Characterized by manic episodes that typically last at least seven days. Depressive episodes usually occur as well and last for at least two weeks.	Manic and depressive	Episodes of depression with mixed features (of both depression and manic symptoms) may also occur.
Bipolar II Disorder	Defined by a pattern of depressive and hypomanic episodes.	Hypomanic and depressive	Absent are full-blown manic episodes that are characteristic of Bipolar I.

Cyclothymia	Characterized by multiple periods of hypomanic symptoms and depressive symptoms, which last at least two years.	No episodes; just hypomanic and depressive **symptoms**.	The hypomanic and depressive symptoms present do not meet the requirements for a hypomanic episode or depressive episode.
Specified and Unspecified	Defined by symptoms of bipolar disorder that do not qualify for the former three types.	N/A	This category includes bipolar disorder symptoms that come from taking prescription medications or those that are genetic.

Now, what exactly is the difference between a manic and hypomanic episode? Let's look back at the definition of bipolar disorder: it is characterized by really high highs and really low lows, right? Well, those highs are the mania. And when we say highs, we don't necessarily mean good or happy highs—but heightened emotions in general. When a person is manic, they typically experience hyperactivity, rapid thoughts, difficulty sleeping, and will often engage in risky, troublesome behavior (e.g., unprotected sex with random partners, excessive drinking or drug use, gambling, etc.). Rarely does hyperactivity transfer over into productivity, but when it does, the individual soon comes crashing back to earth and the superpower they felt ceases to exist. Hypo-manic individuals show the same symptoms, but they're less severe and typically don't hinder one's everyday functioning.

Now, what about the super-low lows? You guessed it—that's where the depressive episodes come in. Depressive epi-sodes are the very opposite of manic episodes: they're char-acterized by low levels of activity and productivity, feelings of hopelessness, and exhaustion. For a deeper look at how it feels to experience a manic or depressive episode, check out the chart on the next page:

People experiencing a manic episode may...	People experiencing a depressive episode may...
• Have a huge amount of energy • Be or feel extremely productive • Have trouble sleeping • Be abnormally talkative • Compare themselves to famous people • Feel overwhelmed with excitement and happiness • Engage in risky behavior like drug use, gambling • Become easily agitated or irritable • Crank out an absurd amount of work in a small amount of time	• Feel down, empty, and/or hopeless • Have a low amount of energy • Have trouble concentrating • Feel tired even after a substantial amount of sleep • Be withdrawn and distant • Lose interest in their favorite activities • Think about death and/or suicide • Stay in bed all day (or even longer) • Withdraw from work, family, or friends

Okay, we're confident that you understand bipolar disorder a little bit better now. You probably even understand it better than most people! But if you want to get into technicalities, or perhaps you're just super curious, feel free to continue reading and review the full DSM criteria for manic episodes and hypomanic episodes:

Criteria for Manic Episodes: Check Your Symptoms

➢ A distinct period of heightened or irritable moods, lasting at least one week.

➢ During this period, three or more of the symptoms below are present and significant:

o Insomnia or hypersomnia nearly every day

o Obvious mental tension and anxiety

o Racing thoughts and distractibility

o Increase in goal-directed activity

o More outgoing and/or talkative

o Decreased need for sleep

o Increased self-esteem

o Excessive risky behavior

➢ The symptoms don't signify a mixed episode.

➢ The disturbance is severe enough to impair the individual in important areas of life or to require hospitalization of the individual to protect him/herself and others.

➢ The symptoms do not stem from the effects of a drug, medication, other treatment, or a different medical condition.

Criteria for Hypomanic Episodes: Check Your Symptoms

> A distinct period of heightened or irritable moods, lasting at least four days.

> During this period, three or more of the symptoms below are present and significant:

  o Increased self-esteem

  o Decreased need for sleep

  o More outgoing and/or talkative

  o Racing thoughts and distractibility

  o Increase in goal-directed behavior

  o Excessive risky behavior

> The episode is a clear change in functioning and does not represent the person's true personality or normal behavior.

> The disturbance is observable and obvious to others.

> The episode is not severe enough to impair the individual in important areas of life or to require hospitalization.

◊ **To read about the importance of self-awareness, turn to the next page**

◊ **To read about the Best Friend Test, turn to page 35**

◊ **To learn about good and bad habits, turn to page 103**

◊ **If you're grieving the loss of a loved one, flip to page 131**

27

Self-Awareness:
The Greatest Agent for Change

I don't want to get too *Eat Pray Love* on you (it's me, Taylor!), but I learned a lot about myself traveling. I learned how to adapt as well as take charge. I learned that I'm good at making others feel comfortable. I learned that I'd rather be in a classroom teaching than outside in a field planting potatoes. I learned that I love sharing my love for soccer. I learned that I despise living out of a suitcase. I learned that I *need* 8 hours of sleep to perform at my best. I learned that my mind is stronger than any doubt or fear. I learned that I can be everything I need and more.

I'm sorry to say I can't send you on a trip to Europe or Africa to replicate my travel experience; however, I will give you a few simpler, cheaper, and perhaps more realistic tips for improving your self-awareness, or in other words, improving your knowledge of your own needs, feelings, motives, and desires. Here are several techniques you can put to the test anytime and anywhere:

1. **Practice everyday mindfulness.**

   If you're not big on meditating, that's alright. Being mindful (though a form of meditation) is a whole different ballgame. All this practice requires is that you intentionally direct your attention to the present moment. Here, try these:

   - Savor each bite of food that you take. Chew slowly.

   - Notice the faint murmur of noises outside your window.

   - Tune into your surroundings on your daily commute. Sights. Smells. Temperature.

   - When someone's talking, actually listen. What are they saying? Feeling?

   Practicing mindfulness will lead to internal revelations, and you'll understand your mind (and others) better than ever before. For more on this, refer to chapter 9 on self-care practices that actually work!

2. **Journal.**

   Journaling is a cure-all: it reduces stress, clarifies thoughts, increases feelings of happiness, improves overall wellbeing, *and* can ultimately help you get to know yourself better.[24] When you write, you take a

---

24 Tams, L. (2013, May 1). Journaling to reduce stress. Michigan State University. Retrieved from http://www.canr.msu.edu/news/journaling_to_reduce_stress

pause from everything else going on and turn your attention inward. However, if you're intimidated by the traditional sense of journaling or you just aren't super into it, here are some simple, speedy options:

Q&A a Day Journal: This modern approach to journaling doesn't demand the same degree of work or commitment. All you do is answer a quick prompt each day in 1-3 lines. Like this:

April 3: Who matters most in your life, right now?

My husband, my parents and my best friend Sam.

One Line a Day Journal: This journal is similar to the previous, in that it is a quick alternative to the more traditional long-hand journaling. In your One Line a Day Journal you simply write down a brief thought each day:

Today, I'm grateful to have finished my project at work and gone to a paint-and-sip art class with my friend Jen.

3. **Ask for feedback.**

The truth is that it's hard to look at yourself objectively. To get around that hurdle, you can ask for feedback from your friends, your family members, your coworkers, so long as you can trust them, and you're sure they have your best interest at heart. Tell them that you're looking for honest and open feedback; that it won't hurt you, but help you learn more about yourself and likely become a better person. Don't shy away from asking questions either; if you need further clarification on something, ask for it! If it's hard for you to admit that something's off or that you need help with this, remind yourself that these people care about you. They want to see you excel in life—and they'll likely jump at the chance to help you do so.

4. **Monitor self-talk.**

   Yep, those mental deceptions are going to come into play again (and again and again). As you know, the way you talk to and feel about yourself has a huge impact on your life. If your self-talk is predominantly negative, you've got to stop those thoughts in their tracks. And start turning them around. See chapter 2.

5. **Listen to your body.**

   Your physical sensations can serve as a reliable source of feedback for how you truly feel. **Is your jaw clenched? Are your palms sweaty? Does your stomach feel tight?** These are telltale signs that you aren't feeling too good about what's happening. For example, if you're deciding whether or not you should accept a job offer and you're experiencing these very sensations, the answer might be a no. Your body is sending you messages, learn to listen to them.

6. **Look at motivations.**

   Why do you do the things you do? Explore this question and you'll discover a whole lot about yourself; it'll unlock a whole new world of information. This was a fun game to play during my time abroad. Whenever I found myself unsure of a decision, I asked myself, "why?"

Why do you want to do that instead of this? Why do you think this is the right decision?

This forced me to dive deeper and better understand my motivations, as well as my fears, my boundaries, my inner workings. Start to ask yourself, "why?" throughout each day and you'll get to know yourself better very soon.

7. **Rediscover your pleasures.**

Life is constantly changing, and we're changing with it. A couple years ago, maybe your favorite pastime was painting, and now, you have little desire to pick up a paintbrush. You'd rather spend that time reading or jogging outside. Similarly, your taste in music has evolved; your favorite song now is different from your favorite song in college (I don't even like the songs I favorited on Spotify a few months ago!). And while it's fun to play the nostalgia game every now and then, you just don't want to listen to Backstreet Boys all day every day. The point is, don't force yourself to stick with old activities you no longer enjoy. Instead, take the time to rediscover what you enjoy *now*.

No, really, let's do it right now. Think about what you really love to do and write those activities down below. Whenever you're bored or restless or in need of some good vibes/inspiration, refer to this list:

- _____
  _____
- _____

- _____
- _____
- _____

8. **Do a daily check-in.**

   Make it a general rule of thumb to check in with yourself throughout each day. Be aware of your thoughts, your feelings, and those physical sensations we touched on earlier. This isn't a time-consuming, nor difficult process: it can involve journaling or just asking yourself a few questions (aloud or in your head). Once this becomes part of your routine, you'll learn to effortlessly monitor yourself all the time. And your self-awareness will continue to improve.

9. **Understand how people change—and that includes you.**

   We briefly touched on this topic when we addressed how our favorite hobbies and music interests are subject to change over time... but that isn't all of it. As we adopt new habits and behaviors, there's a model that illuminates different stages of change we experience. It's called, simply, the Stages of Change Model, which is based on the stages of change developed by Professors of Psychology Prochaska and DiClemente.[25] In any given moment, we fall into one of these 7 stages:

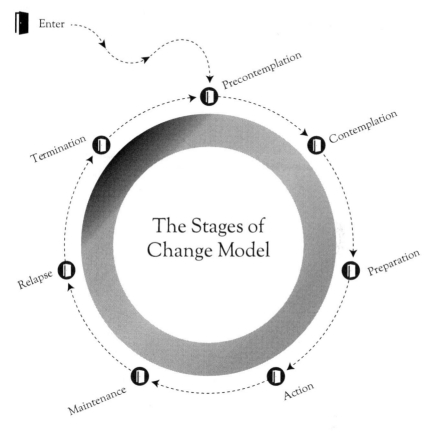

 Exit & re-enter at any stage

25   LaMorte, W. (2018, August 29). The Transtheoretical Model (Stages of Change). Boston University School of Public Health. Retrieved from http://sphweb.bumc.bu.edu/otlt/MPH-Modules/SB/BehavioralChangeTheories/BehavioralChangeTheories6.html

Precontemplation: In this stage of change, you're static. You have yet to identify a change you want to make! You don't want to change, or you're unaware that you need to change.

Contemplation: You've identified a change you want to make. You see how your life might benefit from the change, but at this point you have no timeline in place for when you might begin.

Preparation: You're inching closer and closer to action. You plan to take action toward your change in the near future (within the next 6 months). You might even be taking small steps to get ready, and you're realizing more clearly the impact this change will have on you.

Action: I'm sure you can take a wild guess at what this stage entails. Yep, in this stage, you've started to take action! You're pushing forward and putting your change in place.

Maintenance: In this stage, you've succeeded in implementing the change for at least 6 months, and you're continuing to maintain your new lifestyle.

Relapse: This stage often, but not always, occurs. Here, you start to fall back into old habits, or the ways things were before the change. After this stage, you may choose to go back to "action."

Termination: You have no desire to return to life before you made your important change and you can't even imagine what life would be like if you *didn't* initiate the change in the first place.

Understanding these stages of change (and stopping every now and then to think about which stage you're currently in) will guide you on your self-awareness journey and bring you one step closer to living happier.

When I got back to the states from my adventure abroad, I was in a pure state of bliss. Sure, the beautiful cities in Europe and the countryside in Africa didn't hurt. But my improved understanding and renewed confidence in myself are what enabled me to reach this level of happiness. I'm confident that when you take some time to explore your feelings, rediscover your pleasures, and understand where you are as well as where you want to be, you'll benefit too. And your improved self-awareness will aid your battle with depression.

◊ **To read about how antidepressants can help treat depression, turn the page**

◊ **If you just had a baby and something feels off, flip to page 51**

◊ **If you feel super depressed in the wintertime, turn to page 123**

28

Medications for Depression

In 2017, 12.7% of Americans aged 12 and over reported taking an antidepressant within the last month.[26] People of all sexes, races, and ages take antidepressants to combat depressive feelings. Sometimes they work, sometimes they don't.

Depending on who you are—what you read and what you watch—you might believe that antidepressants defeat depression the way antibiotics kill bacteria or, on the other hand, that they're placebos that do nothing but enrich pharmaceutical companies. Neither is quite right. What's true is that antidepressants *can* work wonders. And when they do, you know it. Like one day, usually several weeks after treatment starts, you feel significantly better—and the improvement lasts, at least as long as you're taking the medication.

---

26   Pratt, L. A., Brody, D. J., & Gu, Q. (2017, August). Antidepressant use among persons aged 12 and over: United states, 2011-2014. Centers for Disease Control and Prevention. Retrieved from https://www.cdc.gov/nchs/products/databriefs/db283.htm

So, what about those side effects? Sure, sometimes there are some not-so-great side effects, like dizziness, headaches, and reduced sex drive. But typically, they're worth the gamble, considering the not-so-great effects of depression.

It's important to consider and discuss your specific situation with a doctor to determine whether antidepressants are right for you. And if they are (or seem to be), you need to have a thorough conversation with the doc about your new pill journey that covers…

- What results to expect and how soon to expect them

- Potential side effects

- Substances you should avoid when taking the meds

- How the meds might interact with other drugs you're taking

- Whether the meds will affect any medical conditions you have

Your primary care physician can prescribe antidepressants, but if possible, at least a few visits with a psychiatrist are typically advised. Psychiatrists have specialized experience with antidepressants and can provide insight into which one will probably work best for you. So, what might you get prescribed? Let's delve into some of the most well-known and widely used antidepressants:

Selective Serotonin Reuptake Inhibitors (SSRIs)

SSRIs are the most commonly prescribed antidepressants, as they come with few side effects (yay), compared to other medications used to treat depression. Potential side effects include drowsiness, nausea, insomnia, and reduced sexual desire or erectile disfunction. SSRIs work by increasing your levels of serotonin, a neurotransmitter in the brain that plays an important part in one's happy, stable mood. To be more specific, they block the reabsorption of serotonin, thus making more serotonin available. Some of the most popular SSRIs (perhaps you've heard of them), are...

Prozac (or fluoxetine): In addition to depression, this is used to treat obsessive compulsive disorder (OCD), bulimia, and panic attacks. It can improve one's mood, sleep quality, energy level, and appetite. And it also works to diminish anxiety, fear, and unwanted thoughts.

Celexa (or citalopram): Celexa is also commonly used to treat the symptoms of depression. Additionally, it has been prescribed to treat alcoholism, binge-eating disorder, anxiety, and OCD.

Serotonin and Noradrenaline Reuptake Inhibitors (SNRIs)

SNRIs are also used to treat depression, as well as other mood disorders, and sometimes attention deficit/hyperactivity disorder (ADHD), anxiety disorders, and OCD. These work by increasing serotonin and norepinephrine (a stress hormone and neurotransmitter) levels, which both play a major role in regulating one's mood. Potential side effects of SNRIs include dizziness, dry mouth, tiredness, and anxiety. The following SNRI might ring a bell…

Cymbalta (or duloxetine): While Cymbalta is used primarily to treat depression and anxiety, it can also relieve nerve pain in people with diabetes, or ongoing pain that comes with conditions like arthritis. This medication works to improve one's mood, appetite, sleep quality, and energy level (much like Prozac).

Effexor (or venlafaxine): This antidepressant can improve mood and energy level, plus it helps to restore interest in everyday living. In addition, Effexor can help relieve symptoms of posttraumatic stress disorder (PTSD), panic disorder, and anxiety.

Atypical Antidepressants

There are some antidepressants that are neither SSRIs nor SNRIs. For example, tricyclic antidepressants and mono-amine oxidase inhibitors (MAOIs) are older categories of antidepressants that, while effective, usually produce a greater number (or severity) of side effects. Hence, these categories are not often prescribed these days, except in special circumstances—like if a client hasn't received a therapeutic benefit from newer medications. In addition, there are other antidepressants used in the treatment of depression that don't fit within any category. These are referred to as atypical antidepressants, and there is one very popular atypical antidepressant you've probably heard of:

> **Wellbutrin** (or bupropion): Wellbutrin is a popular antidepressant, which is also used to help people quit smoking, and has very few side effects. In fact, it doesn't seem to cause the two side effects people are most worried about: weight gain (on Wellbutrin, some people actually lose weight) and loss of sex drive.

This concludes our ultra-basic crash course in antidepressants. Now, go have a talk with your primary care provider or psychiatrist—they can help you determine whether medication is a good treatment option for you, as well as which antidepressant might best serve you.

◊ To read about different approaches to happiness, flip the page

◊ To read about effective self-care practices, turn to page 41

◊ To read about sports fan depression, start on page 145

29

Happiness Squared

"And they lived happily ever after. The end." If only life were like the fairytales we read as kids. All of us are in search of happiness, but often, it somehow evades us. In the bestseller book *Happier: Learn the Secrets to Daily Joy and Lasting Fulfillment,* author and Harvard professor Tal Ben-Shahar identifies four types of people and how they approach happiness and suffering.[27] We wanted to dedicate a chapter to these insights because we think they're pretty profound and can help you make better choices for both your short-term and long-term happiness. Accordingly, here's our take on the four quadrants—four styles—for how we can approach happiness in our lives:

1. YOLOer: Happiness now, pain later.

YOLOers focus on enjoying the present while ignoring potential negative consequences of their actions.

---

27   Ben-Shahar, T. (2007, May 31). Happier: Learn the Secrets to Daily Joy and Lasting Fulfillment. McGraw-Hill Education.

Example: **"**I'm going to eat this entire cake and drink all the martinis!" Sure, you'll enjoy the cake and martinis while you're indulging, but you certainly won't feel too good later. Yikes.

2. Work Horse: Pain now, happiness later.

Work Horses enslave themselves to the present in pursuit of a better future. They are masters of delaying gratification.

Example: "I work 100 hours a week to guarantee I have a great career down the road!" You might work your way up the corporate ladder and enjoy your standing in a few years, but you certainly won't enjoy today or tomorrow or the day after that. You'll likely be stressed out and tired instead.

3. Sad Sack: Pain now, pain later.

Sad Sacks have lost their love for life. A sad sack neither enjoys the moment nor has a sense of future happiness.

Example: "Well, this party sucks, I don't know anybody. I'm going to sit here and just get lonelier." You're not having any fun at the moment, and you're not doing anything to make the rest of the night more enjoyable.

4. Joy Chooser: Happiness now, happiness later.

Joy Choosers live according to the knowledge that the worthiest activities can bring enjoyment in the present and lead to a fulfilling future.

Example: "I'm going to pursue a career that I love! I don't want to dread going to work, and I don't want to be stressed outside of work." You've chosen to do something you enjoy, which will make for a happier you now and later.

For all us visual learners, here's a chart that shows the four quadrants:

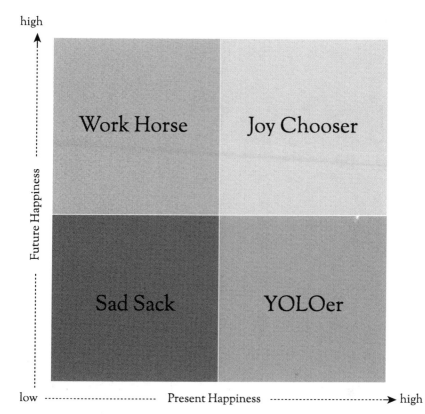

high

Future Happiness

Work Horse | Joy Chooser

Sad Sack | YOLOer

low ---- Present Happiness ----→ high

Now, which happiness quadrant do you fall into? Are you a Work Horse, in that you put yourself through the ringer now so you can enjoy a better future? Or are you a Joy Chooser, in that you always choose to enjoy a present moment that also promises an enjoyable tomorrow?

Consider these million-dollar questions:

Which style do you spend most of your time in? Explain.

_____

_____

_____

_____

Do you ever feel like a Work Horse? (Does it prove valuable to your life?)

_____

_____

_____

_____

Have you ever lived as a YOLOer? (What were the costs and benefits of living this way?)

_____

_____

_____

_____

Have you ever felt like a Sad Sack? (Were you unable to see beyond your current pain?)

_____

_____

_____

_____

_____

Finally, think about when you've been a Joy Chooser... a time when you pursued both present and future benefit!

_____

_____

_____

_____

_____

Let's try a happiness exercise. For the next four days, spend about five minutes a day writing about your experiences living in each of the four styles (most of us spend at least some time in each). Explain the behaviors you engaged in, the emotions you experienced during the behaviors, and the emotions you felt after the positive or negative consequences of your behaviors. Feel free to record the exercise on the following pages:

Date: _____

_____

_____

_____

_____

_____

Date: _____

_____

_____

_____

_____

_____

Date: _____

_____

_____

_____

_____

_____

Date: _____

_____

_____

_____

_____

_____

◊ To read about setting healthy boundaries in your relation-ships, flip the page

◊ If you're on the shy side and need some tips for socializing, turn to page 93

◊ To learn about the dangers of being a loyal sports fan, turn to page 145

30

Setting Healthy Boundaries

Have you ever struggled with being a people-pleaser? Do you tend to overcommit yourself? Yeah, join the club. Many of us give in to the "yes" monster too often. It's almost like "no" is a curse word, or we're reluctant to say it because saying "no," "nada," "can't make it," "can't help you," or "not now" is a sign of being a selfish good-for-nothing jerk. So, we say "yes" instead, even to our own detriment…

Yes, to picking up the extra project at work…
even if you burn out because of it.

Yes, to watching the neighbor's kids…
even when you don't want to.

Yes, to the one-night stand… even if you
know you'll regret it later.

Yes, to lending a friend money… even when
you don't feel good about it.

Just like a physical fence protects what's inside, when you set a healthy boundary, you're protecting yourself from outside forces or influences who want to—purposefully or accidentally—take advantage of you or ask more of you than you're really able to give.

To not have boundaries is to have a stressed-out, frazzled, unhealthy life and can be a contributor to your depression. In other words, you have to learn to say "no" and set limits with the people in your life: your mental wellness depends on it. If this sounds like something you need help with, here are a few tips:

1. **Accept that you're not a superhero.**

   Sorry, but you're not! So, don't put yourself under that kind of pressure. Saying "no" doesn't make you selfish or mean. It means you're human and you had to make a choice that worked for you. Besides, counselors have found that people who do a few things well will find more joy and satisfaction in life than those who try to do too much (ever heard the saying, "Keep the main thing, the main thing"?). So, be realistic about what you can invest your time in. Don't overcommit!

2. **Make your limits known.**

   An invisible fence only works with pets, so let people see your limits. Too often, we don't want to show people our boundaries because, we fear that if we do, they won't respect them anyway. Let this worry go—be straightforward and honest about what you can and can't do. It's far better to say "no" upfront than to say "yes" and then fail to follow through (or follow through at your own detriment).

For example, if you need your weekends for R&R, let people know that you're not going to be available to fill your weekends with favors. You're not the person to call if they need someone to help them move. However, if anyone wants to join you for a glass of wine while you rest and relax, they're welcome to stop by!

3. **Care for yourself.**

If you don't take care of yourself, you can't take care of anyone else. Build time into your schedule to take care of *you*… whether that means reading a book, going for a jog, taking a bubble bath, or playing golf. On that note, make sure you have lots of margin in your schedule. Margin is a grace period from one thing to the next. Too many of us are running 30 minutes late all day because we haven't worked margin into our lives.

4. **Drop the guilt.**

You are not the world's savior. It's not your job to make everyone happy or "fix" all of the problems for those around you. Don't succumb to the pressure of other peoples' needs; evaluate your heart and commit only what you can happily and freely give. The reality is that there will always be people who need something, and if you don't set clear personal boundaries, you will attract them like a magnet.

If your life has been defined or dictated by the needs of others, don't worry. One fencepost at a time, you can set healthy boundaries. As you learn to say "no," you'll begin to better enjoy the relationships in your life (rather than feel drained and used by them). Your new boundaries will free you up to experience freedom and satisfaction in relationships like never before.

◊ To read about the many types of depression, carry on to the next chapter

◊ To read about how your Netflix habits could hurt you, flip to page 97

◊ To evaluate (and improve) different areas of your life, turn to page 117

◊ To read about medications that are used to treat depression, flip to page 171

31

Every Other Kind of Depression

In other chapters, we examined some of the most prevalent forms of depression. We delved into major as well as minor depression, bipolar I and II, postpartum, and seasonal affective disorder. But we aren't finished yet. There are still other kinds of depression out there that vary in severity, symptoms, duration, and cause—some you've likely never heard of before. So, let's dive in, shall we?

Persistent Depressive Disorder

Persistent depressive disorder, often called "dysthymia" or "chronic depression," differs from major depressive disorder in degree and duration. With persistent depressive disorder, the pain and disruption are of a lower intensity and can be described as a general sadness or lack of interest in life.

Criteria for Persistent Depressive Disorder: Check Your Symptoms

One must experience a depressed mood that occurs for most of the day, more days than not, for at least two years (or one year for children and teens). Additionally, the individual must present at least two of the following six symptoms:

> ➤ Poor appetite or overeating
> ➤ Fatigue or loss of energy
> ➤ Disruption of sleep patterns
> ➤ Low self-esteem
> ➤ Feelings of hopelessness
> ➤ Diminished ability to think or concentrate

Additionally, no major depressive episode has been present during the first two years of the disturbance, and the disturbance isn't better explained by major depressive disorder.

Disruptive Mood Dysregulation Disorder

Disruptive mood dysregulation disorder (DMDD) is characterized by severe outbursts of anger or aggression in children and adolescents. While anger and irritability are present in this condition, it goes way beyond being a "moody" child or teen—kids with DMDD suffer with severe impairment.

Criteria for Disruptive Mood Dysregulation Disorder: Check Your Symptoms

An individual who falls between the ages of 6 and 18 must experience the following for a year or longer:

➢ Angry or irritable mood most of the day, nearly every day

➢ Severe outbursts (verbal or behavioral) at least three or more times a week that don't fit with the situation or the child's developmental level

➢ Difficulty functioning due to irritability in more than one area of life (e.g., at home, at school, or with peers)

Premenstrual Dysphoric Disorder

Premenstrual dysphoric disorder is sometimes described as an extreme form of PMS; with depression, irritability, and mood swings leading to impairment of normal functioning in the week before menstruation.

Criteria for Premenstrual Dysphoric Disorder: Check Your Symptoms

In most menstrual cycles during the last year, the individual experienced five or more of the following symptoms during the week before their period, which resolved after their period. Furthermore, the individual *must* experience at least one of the first four symptoms listed here:

➢ Feelings of intense sadness, hopelessness, despair, emptiness
➢ Marked anxiety or tension (i.e., feeling on edge)
➢ Heightened emotions or emotional sensitivity
➢ Persistent anger or irritability
➢ Loss of pleasure in most daily activities
➢ Diminished ability to think or concentrate
➢ Changes in activity levels
➢ Significant weight or appetite changes
➢ Disruption of sleep patterns: insomnia or hypersomnia
➢ Feelings of overwhelm or lack of control
➢ Other physical symptoms such as headaches, bloating, muscle pain, or breast tenderness.

Substance-Induced Depressive Disorder

If you're using substances daily, you may experience substance-induced depressive disorder symptoms as a hangover, tiredness, or the grayness of being without the chemical. And you might not really think of it as depression, but your mood is depressed

Criteria for Substance-Induced Depressive Disorder: Check Your Symptoms

One must present one or both of the following:

> ➤ Depressed mood or loss of interest in most daily activities
> ➤ Marked irritability or an elevated mood

It is also clear from their history, physical examination, or other findings that one of the following is true:

> ➤ The above symptoms developed during or within one month of their substance intoxication or withdrawal
> ➤ The individual's disturbance is rooted in the substance use

Furthermore, the individual's disturbance is not better explained by another mood disorder, and the symptoms cause significant distress or impairment in important areas of life.

Depressive Disorder Due to Another Medical Condition

This is where it gets a little tricky (as if it weren't already tricky). Chronic illness of any kind can bring on depression, which is classified as depressive disorder due to another medical condition. Mental health conditions—anxiety disorder, post-traumatic stress disorder, schizophrenia, schizoaffective disorder, and others—can include depression as a symptom or as a coexisting illness... and because of the complexity of co-morbid conditions, your doctor might struggle to determine which it is. What's most important is that you open up about your depressive feelings and figure out a plan for moving forward with your doctor, even if you think that it's normal to be depressed when you're suffering with another tough illness. All the mental disorders listed above, as well as illnesses like diabetes, lupus, and multiple sclerosis are harder to treat than depression. So, if you can get any sort of relief from the depression, it will make whatever other illness you have easier to bear. To look at the DSM criteria for depressive disorder due to another medical condition, look to the next page.

Criteria for Depressive Disorder Due to Another Medical Condition: Check Your Symptoms

All of the following must be true for an individual to meet diagnostic criteria for depressive disorder due to another medical condition:

> ➤ The individual must experience a period of depressed mood or a diminished interest in all or most daily activities

> ➤ It is clear from the individual's history, physical examination, or other findings that the disturbance is directly related to another medical condition

> ➤ The disturbance is not better explained by another mental disorder

> ➤ The disturbance does not occur exclusively during a state of delirium (or a state of mind characterized by restlessness and incoherence)

> ➤ The disturbance causes the individual significant distress or impairment in important areas of life

Adjustment Disorder

Adjustment disorder is a psychological reaction to a change in circumstances that causes *serious* disruption. Divorce, illness, and unemployment can be triggers... but so can a seemingly exciting milestone like going off to college or getting married. Symptoms include anxiety, sadness, and unhealthy sleeping and eating patterns, but they aren't as severe as they are with major depression. Nor do they stick around as long as they do with dysthymia. People with substance abuse problems or family issues may be susceptible to recurrent adjustment disorders. You can find the DSM criteria on the next page.

Criteria for Adjustment Disorder: Check Your Symptoms

One must experience an identifiable stressor, which brings about emotional or behavioral symptoms within three months of onset of the stressor. Either or both of the following must be true:

> ➢ Distress is out of proportion with expected reactions to the stressor
> ➢ The symptoms are clinically significant, meaning they cause distress or impairment in important areas of functioning.

Additionally, the following must be true:

> ➢ The individual's distress is directly related to the stressor and not better explained by an existing mental health disorder
> ➢ The reaction isn't part of normal bereavement (or grief)
> ➢ Once the stressor is no longer, or the individual has learned to cope, the symptoms subside within six months

Psychotic Depression

Psychotic depression, also known as major depressive disorder with psychotic features, is a rare form of depression that includes psychotic delusions or hallucinations. This disorder demands immediate treatment and close monitoring by a mental health or medical professional.

Criteria for Psychotic Depression: Check Your Symptoms

Individuals with psychotic depression experience severe depressive feelings along with a co-existing psychosis. This psychosis may manifest as hallucinations, delusions, or simply unrealistic experiences. Symptoms might include:

> ➢ Agitation
> ➢ Insomnia
> ➢ Anxiety
> ➢ Intellectual impairment
> ➢ Physical immobility

That concludes our section on "other" types of depression—where to next?

◊ For a much-needed revelation, flip to the next page

◊ To better understand the severity of your depression, flip to page 31

◊ If you need help moving forward after a breakup, turn to page 55

◊ To read about anxiety disorders, turn to page 69

32

It's Okay to Not Be Okay

I'm fine. ← One of the biggest lies you've ever heard, or better yet, told. Instead of facing painful emotions, we do our best to swallow them. We insist that we're fine (when we're absolutely not fine) in hopes of reassuring concerned friends, family, even ourselves. And we continue to go about life as "normal," despite the breakup, the bad news, the setback, whatever we're struggling with at the time. But eventually, all of those feelings come bubbling to the surface and explode in our faces (like so much vomit). Why? Because ignoring, denying, or suppressing emotions, is not the answer. No matter how difficult or inconvenient they may be to accept or experience… if you want to heal, you need to *feel*.

There's been a whole lot of talk in this book about correcting mental deceptions and assuming a positive mindset—which is why we're taking a pause to say this: **It's okay to not be okay.**

We all experience painful emotions. We all get in crappy moods. We all have bad days. Yes, our mission is to help you overcome your depression and get you to a happy, healthy place again—but we aren't miracle workers. We can't guard you from every sucky feeling out there. Sucky feelings aren't rooted in being depressed, but in being human. It kind of comes with the territory. The sooner you accept this, the sooner you can focus on what *is* in your control: how you process these difficult emotions. Here are four basic guidelines…

1. **Pause and reflect.**

   When you find yourself facing a difficult emotion, the first thing you should do is take a moment to think: "What am I feeling? Where am I feeling it?" More often than not, a difficult emotion is accompanied by a physical sensation, such as a tightness in the throat or butterflies in the stomach. Acknowledge these feelings.

2. **Ask yourself, "why?"**

   Take your time in exploring why you feel the way that you do. Why do you feel angry or frustrated? Why are you upset or nervous? Exploring what has triggered these emotions can help you handle them more effectively.

3. **Write it down.**

   Writing your feelings down can also help you come to terms with your feelings and better understand yourself. Not to mention, those journal entries will serve as a great resource for the next time you experience painful emotions.

4. **Open up to a trusted friend.**

   If you feel comfortable doing so, opening up to a trusted friend is another effective way to process emotions. Sometimes just the act of "talking about it" helps.

Alright, now we're going to throw you a "pity party." That's right, we're giving you a free pass to wallow in your pity for a minute. You have our permission to order all the pizza, all the Chinese food in the world, and to eat it from the comfort of your bed. Or hey, doesn't a warm bubble bath with a few candles and relaxing music sound nice? Maybe some simple snuggles on the couch with your dog. Or perhaps even a day's break from work to recollect yourself.

If you read chapter 9 on self-care strategies that actually work, you might have picked up on a few similarities here. Music, snuggles with the pup, mental health day… anything ringing a bell? Yeah, so we might have tricked you… this isn't *exactly* a pity party. It's more like a self-care party.

Do you get the point? It's okay to not be okay. Crap happens to everyone, and you deserve to feel a little sorry for yourself from time to time. But you ultimately have to focus on what *is* in your control, such as how you care for yourself during those difficult times. In honor of that, let's write down a few go-to feel-good activities for when you just want to throw yourself a big ole' pity party:

1. _____

   _____

2. _____

   _____

3. _____

   _____

4. _____

   _____

5. _____

   _____

Awesome! Now, hopefully you have a new perspective on what a "pity party" entails... no, no one's telling you that you can't pig out on some pizza, Chinese food, ice cream, or all of the above (we would *never*). But we are saying that you can take additional actions—that you'll thoroughly enjoy—to take extra good care of yourself when you aren't feeling your best.

◊ For a final discussion about defeating your depression, flip to the next page

◊ If you're pregnant and feel awful, turn to page 51

◊ To read about the irrational stories we tell ourselves, turn to page 75

◊ To learn about how you can create healthy habits, turn to page 103

33

Leaving Depression Behind

So, have you left your depression behind? Your answer might be no, and that's okay—because overcoming depression is a committed process. We stick by what we said at the start of this book: we can't promise to cure you of depression by the time you've finished reading, but the exercises and insights that fill these pages are meant to help you begin the process. If you've learned one thing from reading this book, we hope you've learned how to change your mental deceptions that are literally causing or at least exacerbating your depression. Now, you have the ability to:

a) Stop.

b) Write down your thoughts.

c) Identify when they're wrong.

d) Change them.

Leaving depression behind is this process of reframing negative self-talk and engaging in positive self-talk. It's choosing to prioritize self-care. It's understanding that a breakup isn't the end of the world but a new beginning. It's allowing yourself to experience the beauty that is human connection. It's shaking bad habits and creating healthy ones. It's admitting that you need help, seeking help, and accepting help. It's conquering the monsters under your bed, or the harmful narratives you tell yourself. It's understanding that grief stems from the most powerful emotion we can experience: love. It's taking a good, hard look at yourself and understanding which area of your life could use some work. And it's accepting that some days you just won't be okay—and that's okay.

Leaving depression behind is not a one-day or even a one-month process. Even with the help of a therapist it can take a while. But it always begins the same way: it begins with you choosing to face and solve the problem. We hope this book helps. And we wish you luck, healing, and happiness on your journey.

Your Daily Mood Logs

*On the next 20 pages, you'll find your daily mood logs. Remember, these are designed to provide you with some much-needed perspective when your mental deceptions take over. If you need a refresher on how to complete a daily mood log, take a look at chapter 3!

Date: _____

Event:
Feelings:

Negative Thoughts	Mental Deception	How true? Then/Now	Alternative Positive Thoughts	How true?	How do I feel now?

Date: _____

Event:
Feelings:

Negative Thoughts	Mental Deception	How true? Then/Now	Alternative Positive Thoughts	How true?	How do I feel now?

Date: _____

Event:
Feelings:

Negative Thoughts	Mental Deception	How true? Then/Now	Alternative Positive Thoughts	How true?	How do I feel now?

Date: _____

Event:
Feelings:

Negative Thoughts	Mental Deception	How true? Then/Now	Alternative Positive Thoughts	How true?	How do I feel now?

Date: _____

Event:
Feelings:

Negative Thoughts	Mental Deception	How true? Then/Now	Alternative Positive Thoughts	How true?	How do I feel now?

Date: _____

Event:
Feelings:

Negative Thoughts	Mental Deception	How true? Then/Now	Alternative Positive Thoughts	How true?	How do I feel now?

Date: _____

Event:
Feelings:

Negative Thoughts	Mental Deception	How true? Then/Now	Alternative Positive Thoughts	How true?	How do I feel now?

Date: _____

| Event: |
| Feelings: |

Negative Thoughts	Mental Deception	How true? Then/Now	Alternative Positive Thoughts	How true?	How do I feel now?

Date: _____

Event:
Feelings:

Negative Thoughts	Mental Deception	How true? Then/Now	Alternative Positive Thoughts	How true?	How do I feel now?

Date: _____

Event:
Feelings:

Negative Thoughts	Mental Deception	How true? Then/Now	Alternative Positive Thoughts	How true?	How do I feel now?

Date: _____

Event:
Feelings:

Negative Thoughts	Mental Deception	How true? Then/Now	Alternative Positive Thoughts	How true?	How do I feel now?

Date: _____

| Event: |
| Feelings: |

Negative Thoughts	Mental Deception	How true? Then/Now	Alternative Positive Thoughts	How true?	How do I feel now?

Date: _____

Event:
Feelings:

Negative Thoughts	Mental Deception	How true? Then/Now	Alternative Positive Thoughts	How true?	How do I feel now?

Date: _____

Event:
Feelings:

Negative Thoughts	Mental Deception	How true? Then/Now	Alternative Positive Thoughts	How true?	How do I feel now?

Date: _____

Event:
Feelings:

Negative Thoughts	Mental Deception	How true? Then/Now	Alternative Positive Thoughts	How true?	How do I feel now?

Date: _____

Event:
Feelings:

Negative Thoughts	Mental Deception	How true? Then/Now	Alternative Positive Thoughts	How true?	How do I feel now?

Date: _____

Event:

Feelings:

Negative Thoughts	Mental Deception	How true? Then/Now	Alternative Positive Thoughts	How true?	How do I feel now?

Date: _____

| Event: |
| Feelings: |

Negative Thoughts	Mental Deception	How true? Then/Now	Alternative Positive Thoughts	How true?	How do I feel now?

Date: _____

Event:
Feelings:

Negative Thoughts	Mental Deception	How true? Then/Now	Alternative Positive Thoughts	How true?	How do I feel now?

Date: _____

Event:
Feelings:

Negative Thoughts	Mental Deception	How true? Then/Now	Alternative Positive Thoughts	How true?	How do I feel now?

Date: _____

Event:
Feelings:

Negative Thoughts	Mental Deception	How true? Then/Now	Alternative Positive Thoughts	How true?	How do I feel now?

Date: _____

| Event: |
| Feelings: |

Negative Thoughts	Mental Deception	How true? Then/Now	Alternative Positive Thoughts	How true?	How do I feel now?

Date: _____

| Event: |
| Feelings: |

Negative Thoughts	Mental Deception	How true? Then/Now	Alternative Positive Thoughts	How true?	How do I feel now?

Date: _____

Event:
Feelings:

Negative Thoughts	Mental Deception	How true? Then/Now	Alternative Positive Thoughts	How true?	How do I feel now?

Date: _____

Event:
Feelings:

Negative Thoughts	Mental Deception	How true? Then/Now	Alternative Positive Thoughts	How true?	How do I feel now?

Date: _____

| Event: |
| Feelings: |

Negative Thoughts	Mental Deception	How true? Then/Now	Alternative Positive Thoughts	How true?	How do I feel now?

Date: _____

Event:
Feelings:

Negative Thoughts	Mental Deception	How true? Then/Now	Alternative Positive Thoughts	How true?	How do I feel now?

Date: _____

Event:
Feelings:

Negative Thoughts	Mental Deception	How true? Then/Now	Alternative Positive Thoughts	How true?	How do I feel now?

Date: _____

Event:
Feelings:

Negative Thoughts	Mental Deception	How true? Then/Now	Alternative Positive Thoughts	How true?	How do I feel now?

Date: _____

Event:

Feelings:

Negative Thoughts	Mental Deception	How true? Then/Now	Alternative Positive Thoughts	How true?	How do I feel now?

Date: _____

Event:
Feelings:

Negative Thoughts	Mental Deception	How true? Then/Now	Alternative Positive Thoughts	How true?	How do I feel now?

Date: _____

| Event: |
| Feelings: |

Negative Thoughts	Mental Deception	How true? Then/Now	Alternative Positive Thoughts	How true?	How do I feel now?

Date: _____

Event:
Feelings:

Negative Thoughts	Mental Deception	How true? Then/Now	Alternative Positive Thoughts	How true?	How do I feel now?

Date: _____

Event:
Feelings:

Negative Thoughts	Mental Deception	How true? Then/Now	Alternative Positive Thoughts	How true?	How do I feel now?

Date: _____

Event:
Feelings:

Negative Thoughts	Mental Deception	How true? Then/Now	Alternative Positive Thoughts	How true?	How do I feel now?

Date: _____

Event:
Feelings:

Negative Thoughts	Mental Deception	How true? Then/Now	Alternative Positive Thoughts	How true?	How do I feel now?

Date: _____

Event:
Feelings:

Negative Thoughts	Mental Deception	How true? Then/Now	Alternative Positive Thoughts	How true?	How do I feel now?

Date: _____

Event:
Feelings:

Negative Thoughts	Mental Deception	How true? Then/Now	Alternative Positive Thoughts	How true?	How do I feel now?

Weekly Depression Quizzes

*On the next several pages, you'll find 10 depression quizzes. Complete one each week (and make sure you write the date/time for each!), so you can keep track of your depression symptoms. After you've rated the 15 statements that make up the quiz and you've tallied your score, refer back to this chart. **Remember, this is not a medical or diagnostic tool. Diagnosis can only be provided by a licensed medical or mental health professional.**

Score	Severity of Depression
0-5	Likely not depressed
6-10	Slightly depressed
11-20	Mildly depressed
21-30	Moderately depressed
31-45	Majorly depressed

Date: _____ Time: _____

Not at all	0
Some of the time	1
A good bit of the time	2
Most or all of the time	3

1. I feel unhappy and sometimes even miserable.	
2. My future isn't looking too bright.	
3. I don't feel like I have much to offer.	
4. I toss and turn in my sleep at night.	
5. I have a hard time sleeping in general.	
6. When comparing myself to others, I feel less than.	
7. I'm very self-critical and often take on blame.	
8. I've lost interest in things that used to make me happy.	
9. I'm more indecisive than normal.	
10. I feel out of touch with my closest friends and family.	
11. I have to really push myself to get anything done.	
12. My appetite/eating habits have changed for the worse.	
13. I feel tired even after I get a good amount of sleep.	
14. My life is looking and feeling pretty empty.	
15. Sometimes I think the world would be better off without me.	

Total Score: _____

Date: _____ Time: _____

Not at all	0
Some of the time	1
A good bit of the time	2
Most or all of the time	3

1. I feel unhappy and sometimes even miserable.	
2. My future isn't looking too bright.	
3. I don't feel like I have much to offer.	
4. I toss and turn in my sleep at night.	
5. I have a hard time sleeping in general.	
6. When comparing myself to others, I feel less than.	
7. I'm very self-critical and often take on blame.	
8. I've lost interest in things that used to make me happy.	
9. I'm more indecisive than normal.	
10. I feel out of touch with my closest friends and family.	
11. I have to really push myself to get anything done.	
12. My appetite/eating habits have changed for the worse.	
13. I feel tired even after I get a good amount of sleep.	
14. My life is looking and feeling pretty empty.	
15. Sometimes I think the world would be better off without me.	

Total Score: _____

Date: _____ Time: _____

Not at all	0
Some of the time	1
A good bit of the time	2
Most or all of the time	3

1. I feel unhappy and sometimes even miserable.	
2. My future isn't looking too bright.	
3. I don't feel like I have much to offer.	
4. I toss and turn in my sleep at night.	
5. I have a hard time sleeping in general.	
6. When comparing myself to others, I feel less than.	
7. I'm very self-critical and often take on blame.	
8. I've lost interest in things that used to make me happy.	
9. I'm more indecisive than normal.	
10. I feel out of touch with my closest friends and family.	
11. I have to really push myself to get anything done.	
12. My appetite/eating habits have changed for the worse.	
13. I feel tired even after I get a good amount of sleep.	
14. My life is looking and feeling pretty empty.	
15. Sometimes I think the world would be better off without me.	

Total Score: _____

Date: _____ Time: _____

Not at all	0
Some of the time	1
A good bit of the time	2
Most or all of the time	3

1. I feel unhappy and sometimes even miserable.	
2. My future isn't looking too bright.	
3. I don't feel like I have much to offer.	
4. I toss and turn in my sleep at night.	
5. I have a hard time sleeping in general.	
6. When comparing myself to others, I feel less than.	
7. I'm very self-critical and often take on blame.	
8. I've lost interest in things that used to make me happy.	
9. I'm more indecisive than normal.	
10. I feel out of touch with my closest friends and family.	
11. I have to really push myself to get anything done.	
12. My appetite/eating habits have changed for the worse.	
13. I feel tired even after I get a good amount of sleep.	
14. My life is looking and feeling pretty empty.	
15. Sometimes I think the world would be better off without me.	

Total Score: _____

Date: _____ Time: _____

Not at all	0
Some of the time	1
A good bit of the time	2
Most or all of the time	3

1. I feel unhappy and sometimes even miserable.	
2. My future isn't looking too bright.	
3. I don't feel like I have much to offer.	
4. I toss and turn in my sleep at night.	
5. I have a hard time sleeping in general.	
6. When comparing myself to others, I feel less than.	
7. I'm very self-critical and often take on blame.	
8. I've lost interest in things that used to make me happy.	
9. I'm more indecisive than normal.	
10. I feel out of touch with my closest friends and family.	
11. I have to really push myself to get anything done.	
12. My appetite/eating habits have changed for the worse.	
13. I feel tired even after I get a good amount of sleep.	
14. My life is looking and feeling pretty empty.	
15. Sometimes I think the world would be better off without me.	

Total Score: _____

Date: _____ Time: _____

Not at all	0
Some of the time	1
A good bit of the time	2
Most or all of the time	3

1. I feel unhappy and sometimes even miserable.	
2. My future isn't looking too bright.	
3. I don't feel like I have much to offer.	
4. I toss and turn in my sleep at night.	
5. I have a hard time sleeping in general.	
6. When comparing myself to others, I feel less than.	
7. I'm very self-critical and often take on blame.	
8. I've lost interest in things that used to make me happy.	
9. I'm more indecisive than normal.	
10. I feel out of touch with my closest friends and family.	
11. I have to really push myself to get anything done.	
12. My appetite/eating habits have changed for the worse.	
13. I feel tired even after I get a good amount of sleep.	
14. My life is looking and feeling pretty empty.	
15. Sometimes I think the world would be better off without me.	

Total Score: _____

Date: _____ Time: _____

Not at all	0
Some of the time	1
A good bit of the time	2
Most or all of the time	3

1. I feel unhappy and sometimes even miserable.	
2. My future isn't looking too bright.	
3. I don't feel like I have much to offer.	
4. I toss and turn in my sleep at night.	
5. I have a hard time sleeping in general.	
6. When comparing myself to others, I feel less than.	
7. I'm very self-critical and often take on blame.	
8. I've lost interest in things that used to make me happy.	
9. I'm more indecisive than normal.	
10. I feel out of touch with my closest friends and family.	
11. I have to really push myself to get anything done.	
12. My appetite/eating habits have changed for the worse.	
13. I feel tired even after I get a good amount of sleep.	
14. My life is looking and feeling pretty empty.	
15. Sometimes I think the world would be better off without me.	

Total Score: _____

Date: _____ Time: _____

Not at all	0
Some of the time	1
A good bit of the time	2
Most or all of the time	3

1. I feel unhappy and sometimes even miserable.	
2. My future isn't looking too bright.	
3. I don't feel like I have much to offer.	
4. I toss and turn in my sleep at night.	
5. I have a hard time sleeping in general.	
6. When comparing myself to others, I feel less than.	
7. I'm very self-critical and often take on blame.	
8. I've lost interest in things that used to make me happy.	
9. I'm more indecisive than normal.	
10. I feel out of touch with my closest friends and family.	
11. I have to really push myself to get anything done.	
12. My appetite/eating habits have changed for the worse.	
13. I feel tired even after I get a good amount of sleep.	
14. My life is looking and feeling pretty empty.	
15. Sometimes I think the world would be better off without me.	

Total Score: _____

Date: _____ Time: _____

Not at all	0
Some of the time	1
A good bit of the time	2
Most or all of the time	3

1. I feel unhappy and sometimes even miserable.	
2. My future isn't looking too bright.	
3. I don't feel like I have much to offer.	
4. I toss and turn in my sleep at night.	
5. I have a hard time sleeping in general.	
6. When comparing myself to others, I feel less than.	
7. I'm very self-critical and often take on blame.	
8. I've lost interest in things that used to make me happy.	
9. I'm more indecisive than normal.	
10. I feel out of touch with my closest friends and family.	
11. I have to really push myself to get anything done.	
12. My appetite/eating habits have changed for the worse.	
13. I feel tired even after I get a good amount of sleep.	
14. My life is looking and feeling pretty empty.	
15. Sometimes I think the world would be better off without me.	

Total Score: _____

Date: _____ Time: _____

Not at all	0
Some of the time	1
A good bit of the time	2
Most or all of the time	3

1. I feel unhappy and sometimes even miserable.	
2. My future isn't looking too bright.	
3. I don't feel like I have much to offer.	
4. I toss and turn in my sleep at night.	
5. I have a hard time sleeping in general.	
6. When comparing myself to others, I feel less than.	
7. I'm very self-critical and often take on blame.	
8. I've lost interest in things that used to make me happy.	
9. I'm more indecisive than normal.	
10. I feel out of touch with my closest friends and family.	
11. I have to really push myself to get anything done.	
12. My appetite/eating habits have changed for the worse.	
13. I feel tired even after I get a good amount of sleep.	
14. My life is looking and feeling pretty empty.	
15. Sometimes I think the world would be better off without me.	

Total Score: _____

About the Authors

AJ Centore PhD

Anthony (AJ) Centore Ph.D. is Founder and CEO at Thriveworks—a counseling practice, focused on premium client care, with 85+ locations across the US. He is Private Practice Consultant for the American Counseling Association, columnist for Counseling Today magazine, and Author of How to Thrive in Counseling Private Practice. AJ is a multistate Licensed Professional Counselor and has been quoted in national media sources including The Boston Globe, Chicago Tribune, and CBS Sunday Morning.

Taylor Bennett

Taylor Bennett is a staff writer at Thriveworks. She devotes herself to distributing important information related to mental health and wellbeing, publishing mental health news and self-improvement tips daily. She received her bachelor's degree in multimedia journalism, with minors in professional writing and leadership from Virginia Tech.

Acknowledgements

Lynn Chosiad, PhD	Heidi Faust, LPC	Kerri Harris
Ellie Jeanes	Shelby Keye	Fredrick Marckini
Andrew Milacci, PhD	Fred Milacci, EdD	Charity Minerva
Ryan Neace, LPC	Lauren Neely	Brooke Pfeiffer
Anastasia Reuss	Amber Shimel, MSW	Joshua Straub, PhD

A special thank you to our friends, family members, and colleagues who took the time to read our first draft of *Leaving Depression Behind: An Interactive, Choose Your Path Book*. This book would not have been possible without your help and guidance.

Made in the USA
Columbia, SC
27 June 2020